PARABLES
REMIX

D1296070

STUDY GUIDE

PARABLES
REMIX

**18 SHORT FILMS
BASED ON THE
PARABLES
OF JESUS**

STEW REDWINE WITH CRAIG MACELVAIN

ZONDERVAN®

ZONDERVAN.com/
AUTHORTRACKER
follow your favorite authors

ZONDERVAN

Parables Remix Study Guide
Copyright © 2012 by Stew Redwine

This title is also available as a Zondervan ebook. Visit www.zondervan.com/ebooks.

Requests for information should be addressed to:

Zondervan, *Grand Rapids, Michigan* 49530

ISBN 978-0-310-69237-9

Cover design: Ron Huizinga
Interior design: Matthew Van Zomeren

Printed in the United States of America

12 13 14 15 16 17 18 19 /DCI/ 20 19 18 17 16 15 14 13 12 11 10 9 8 7 6 5 4 3 2 1

CONTENTS

INTRODUCTION

We all have been guilty at times of unnecessarily shrouding the most ancient and quite mundane human practice of storytelling in a cloak of mystery. There are even those who insist on referring to stories as a proper-noun-capital-S story instead of the common noun it is. But a story is a simple thing, an account of events surrounding a contest of wills. Every day we all tell stories to and with our fellow creatures. I don't think it calls Jesus' deity into question to suppose he told stories in the same way we do.

Even though one third of Jesus' recorded teachings are in the form of a parable, most of us would be hard pressed to produce a list of them beyond "The Prodigal Son" and "The Good Samaritan." When the parables are taught today, they're often treated as an aspect of Jesus' preaching, or considered his creative outlet for when he wasn't talking about the serious stuff. But that is to downplay the vital role they played in his overall ministry.

When Jesus first told his parables on those blistering hot Palestinian days, he was perceived as part political activist and part performance artist. People traveled great distances and missed meals to hear his stories and see his miracles. The mystery of Jesus' humanity comes out in his stories. Like us, when Jesus told a story he was relating to others by sharing events inspired by his life experiences: childhood memories, late-night conversations with friends, a remark he overhead in passing at the market, the taste of a freshly picked fig. Just think ... the day before Jesus told the Parable of the Prodigal Son for the first

> Jesus' parables are stories about everyday people and events told in a way to make a point about everyday people and events.

time, he may have been sitting among the cedars and happened to see an old man running to meet someone in the distance, who very well could have been his long-lost son.

Being fully man also means Jesus must have faced the same challenges and enjoyed the elation of telling a good story that we do. Sometimes it is easy to remember Jesus' humanity solely in the terms that he was tempted and never sinned. But being human involves much more than avoiding temptation. Some of Jesus' stories were great; some of them likely fell flat. So, whatever else you take away from this study, remember this: Jesus was fully human just like you. When you find inspiration in your life to keep going, to love, to laugh, and just stand in the sun and enjoy the warmth, you are taking part in the one theme that runs through all the parables. Jesus' parables are stories about everyday people and events told in a way to make a point about everyday people and events.

MORE QUESTIONS THAN ANSWERS

Jesus' stories were captivating, mysterious, and grounded in the politically super charged day-to-day existence of his audience. And people still left with more questions than answers. I once showed a few of the *Parables Remix* short films to a teenage couple who were blasé about God. At the end of the last short film, the boy turned to me and said, "I don't get it; what are you trying to say?" He had assumed there had to be a catch, an ironclad take-it-or-leave-it message contained in the films. I could tell he was frustrated; and many times, so were those listening to Jesus' parables for the first time. He asked me about the original parables and I read them from the Bible. He then said, "Well, Jesus didn't explain it either."

This response to Jesus' parables is not uncommon. Jesus has always been surrounded by questions. At the beginning of Jesus' life on earth, there were questions. "What child is this?" At the end of his life, there were questions. "Are you the king of the Jews?" At his ascension, there were questions. "Lord, are you at this time going to restore the kingdom to Israel?" and "Why do you stand here looking into the sky?" In the same way, Jesus' parables make us think and ask questions. Questions have a way of driving us to God, because a question begs to be answered. And the real answer, the best answer, the only answer, is a personal relationship with our Father.

He did not say anything to them without using a parable. But when he was alone with his own disciples, he explained everything. (Mark 4:34)

You are in very good company when you tell stories that cause people to ask questions. Instead of taking a lesson or truth from Scripture and insisting on your audience repeating back a pat answer, you can share stories that cause them to ponder the hard questions, such as Pilate's "What is truth?" Don't be afraid of stories with more questions at the end than answers. Those questions are how a relationship can develop between the storyteller and the audience. You really can't lose. Keep telling stories and savor every question asked.

THE FOUR PILLARS OF *PARABLES REMIX*

Here are a few specifics to recognize about this study before you jump in:

1. **We have a finite collection of parables.**
   The scope of *Parables Remix* is by no means intended to be a definitive collection. For two millennia biblical scholars have debated how many parables Jesus told. This difference in opinion depends largely on how scholars choose to interpret the Hebrew word *mashal* that is commonly translated as "parable." Though the gospel writers and Jesus were speaking and writing in another language, when discussing parables they were referencing the richly defined word *mashal* found in the Hebrew scriptures of their day. In Hebrew *mashal* is defined as a riddle, taunt, dark saying, lesson, or story. Like most Eastern languages, Hebrew contains words that are rich with meaning. Different scholars use different definitions, hence a different number of parables.

2. **Our films are narrative.**
   Parables Remix films are a narrative account of connected events. Simply put, each short film is a story. A story is any account of connected events centered on a conflict that is resolved, leaving something or someone absolutely and irreversibly changed. Jesus' parables often leave readers with an absolute change they might not like. Nonetheless, a conflict has been resolved and irreversible change is the result. A perfect example is "The Parable of The Rich Fool" (Luke 12:16–21), summed up in one sentence: The

man who has it all dies. An absolute and irreversible change, for sure! So, in *A Few Weeks Later*, the film based on that parable, we explore how the spouse of the rich fool may have dealt with the mountain of possessions left behind by his dearly departed wife.

3. **Our films are descriptive, not prescriptive.**

We produce descriptive short films, intended to cause the viewer to engage with the story and ask questions. In Robert Farrar Capon's *Kingdom, Grace, Judgment*, he sums up our approach perfectly:

> "For to him who has, more will be given; and from him who has not, even what he has will be taken away" (Matthew 13:12). This seems to me to be one of those hard sayings of Jesus that cries out, not for a prescriptive interpretation, but for a descriptive one. Jesus, though he could be taken as issuing a statement about what God will do to reward or punish those who hear the parables, seems to be more reasonably understood as giving a description of the way things are.

4. **Our films point back to Scripture.**

Jesus told many parables. We are adapting eighteen of them. We do not intend our collection to replace Scripture but to point back to Jesus' original parables. Jesus was and is the light of the world. He is the medium by which God's light shines on all of those in the shadow of death. Jesus spoke in parables during his time on earth. Several hundred years later, Christians spoke with stained glass. Light traveling through the glass illuminated the vibrant colors and retold Jesus' original stories to a new audience. Several hundred years after stained glass came the camera. With *Parables Remix* we once again endeavor to illuminate understanding of Jesus' original parables in contemporary terms using glass and light.

Stew Redwine[1]
June 2012

---

1. This study guide is written from Stew's perspective. Craig MacElvain, a pastor and long-time supporter of the material, helped with the interpretive, cultural, application, and questions sections.

HOW TO USE THIS STUDY

Parables Remix is a cutting-edge teaching tool designed to illuminate understanding by entertaining and engaging the heart—whether used as a part of a sermon or class, by a small group or an individual. Authentic, accurate, simply stated, and profoundly moving, the eighteen short films (each five to ten minutes long) connect in ways words alone cannot.

Each session of this study guide complements the video component with:

- Complete Bible text of the parable
- Group discussion or individual reflection questions
- Pertinent cultural background notes on first-century Israel
- Interesting behind-the-scenes information about the related film with a spiritual tie-in
- Introductory and closing thoughts
- Between-sessions life application activities

Helpful icons will guide your progress through each session:

♡ **PRAY**—Ask God what he wants to reveal to you or your group through this particular parable.

◉ **WATCH**—Watch the short film based on the parable.

📖 **READ**—Read the original parable (NIV text provided).

◯ **DISCUSS**—Discuss the short film and the original parable.

🔄 **REPEAT**—Repeat the process in the same meeting or at your next gathering, watching a different parable or the same one. You may be surprised that many people in your group want to watch the same short film over and over again.

Study *Parables Remix* chronologically or in any order that works for you and your group. Because each film is stand-alone, *Parables Remix* is also ideal for fill-in meetings, retreats, or other special gatherings.

THE **PARABLE** OF THE **GOOD SAMARITAN**

SCRIPTURE: **LUKE 10:30–37**
FILM: *BUEN VECINO*

♡ PRAY TOGETHER

INTRODUCTION

The Parable of the Good Samaritan is perhaps the most popular of Jesus' parables. It has big production value, the villains are religious figures, and the hero is unlikely, to say the least. There's plenty of drama too — robbery, violence, rescue, suspense, and grace. But in *Buen Vecino*, nobody's life is at stake ... there isn't even a robbery.

Randall Wallace, the screenwriter of *Braveheart*, said, "I never let facts get in the way of the truth." This parable communicates many things, but fundamentally the story rests on the truth that Christ calls us to help others. And in making *Buen Vecino* (which means "good neighbor" in Spanish) contemporary to our culture, the film explores our work life and occupational relationships. The employees' striped shirts (which can be hard on the eyes) symbolize the dizzying experience we often feel at work. *Buen Vecino* explores a day when things fall apart around us, vacuums interrupt us, and wheelbarrows get dumped in our pools (or cubicles or whatever). Those (hopefully) rare, disastrous days can cause us to feel as though our very lives are at stake.

👁 WATCH THE FILM *BUEN VECINO*

📖 READ THE PARABLE OF THE GOOD SAMARITAN

[30] In reply Jesus said: "A man was going down from Jerusalem to Jericho, when he was attacked by robbers. They stripped him of his clothes, beat him and went away, leaving him half dead. [31] A priest happened to be going down the same road, and when he saw the man, he passed by on the other side. [32] So too, a Levite, when he came to the place and saw him, passed by on the other side. [33] But a Samaritan, as he traveled, came where the man was; and when he saw him, he took pity on him. [34] He went to him and bandaged his wounds, pouring on oil and wine. Then he put the man on his own donkey, brought him to an inn and took care of him. [35] The next day he took out two denarii and gave them to the innkeeper. 'Look after him,' he said, 'and when I return, I will reimburse you for any extra expense you may have.'

[36] "Which of these three do you think was a neighbor to the man who fell into the hands of robbers?"

[37] The expert in the law replied, "The one who had mercy on him." Jesus told him, "Go and do likewise."

Luke 10:30–37

CULTURAL BACKGROUND

In the Good Samaritan parable, Jesus used familiar images to hook his listeners. The road from "Jerusalem to Jericho" was actually the super-highway of its day—a forty-mile stretch well known for two things: (1) a generous population of priests on their way back and forth from Jerusalem to fulfill their priestly duties; and (2) danger, particularly along one stretch known as *adodim* (which means "blood"—a refer-ence to the often-violent muggings in that area). Jesus' scenario cer-tainly rang true in the ears of his first-century hearers.

Likewise, Jesus intentionally used the image of a Samaritan for impact. Samaritans were hated by the Jews and seen as both heretics and half-breeds. However, this Samaritan goes out of his way to care for the victim. The "two denarii" the Samaritan gives the innkeeper would probably have covered expenses for two to three weeks. Com-mentators through the ages have disagreed on the meaning of this parable. Some have even contended that it's not a parable at all, but rather an extended allegory. They saw the road from Jerusalem to Jericho as the road from Eden to Babel, and that sin has allowed the devil to rob and beat us, leaving us "half dead" by the roadside. To many, Jesus represents the Good Samaritan (he was even accused of being a Samaritan by the Pharisees—see John 8:48).

Jesus has come to rescue the lost and broken—especially the outcasts. He cares for our wounds and even pays the price for our healing. Critics of this interpretation say it overspiritualizes the parable and misses the fundamental point of being a true "neighbor" to all.

DISCUSS THE FILM AND ORIGINAL PARABLE

1. *Buen Vecino* means "good neighbor" in Spanish. What are some of the similarities you see between *Buen Vecino* and the Parable of the Good Samaritan?

2. In what way do you act like a "priest" or a "Levite"? How do we often "pass by" people in our lives? What is Jesus trying to teach us in this parable?

3. What were some of the costs incurred by the Samaritan in the story? What did it cost Magdelena to help in *Buen Vecino*? What are the "costs" that keep you from loving those in need with grace and compassion?

4. The Samaritan in the film is a loud non-English speaking Hispanic hotel maid. If Jesus told this parable today to a church audience, whom might he choose? Who would be most offensive to you?

5. Who would be the last person you would want to help you? How is God challenging you to think of that person as your neighbor?

BEHIND THE SCENES

We only had one chance to dump that wheelbarrow full of dirt in the pool. Seriously, that was it. We were on a tight schedule and had to move on to the next scene in the morning. It was the last shot of the day and everyone was on point. Our first assistant camera person, Laurel, lowered the slate into the shot, called out "Take one and only," and clapped the slate. I held my breath and steadied my camera as if the very existence of life on earth depended on the next few seconds. It was nerve racking to say the least.

And as you saw, we got the shot.

Sometimes it feels like life is a "one and only" encounter. We'll only have this one chance to help this person, or say this thing, or do something about this tragedy. In one sense, that is kind of true. But in another, we live in a world infused with the grace of God, and he is making all things new. Every day we get to choose whether we'll honor the Lord's command to "love your neighbor as yourself."

CLOSING THOUGHTS

And who is my neighbor? This is possibly the most important question asked of Jesus during his life on earth. And the answer Jesus gives in the Parable of the Good Samaritan is equally significant. Jesus shifts the emphasis of the question from generating criteria by which you determine "who is and who is not your neighbor" to what is required in order to define yourself as a neighbor. Simply put, you are a neighbor when you have mercy on your fellow man. By directly linking the word *neighbor* with a particular action that demands a recipient, Jesus perfectly harmonizes his answer with one of the many beautiful melodies resonating throughout the Scriptures: *You are not alone.* From the Ten Commandments to the Beatitudes, the Bible represents the human-to-God relationship in light of how we behave in community with others. As soon as you take away your fellow man from your theology, your foot has set upon a very slippery slope that inevitably ends in the quagmire of Christian nihilism. We were created to live in community with God and our fellow man, not alone. And what determines whether or not our fellow man is our neighbor is not race, gender, culture, geography, or even religion. The single determining factor for whether or not someone is our neighbor is *how we treat them.* If I stand back and ask myself who qualifies as my neighbor, I am missing the point. The Parable of the Good Samaritan makes this perfectly clear. We don't get the luxury of deciding who is and who is not our neighbor before we decide to have mercy on them. The Samaritan was the man's neighbor *because* he had mercy on him.

Go and do likewise.

> He prayeth best, who loveth best
> All things both great and small;
> For the dear God who loveth us,
> He made and loveth all.

> From *The Rime of the Ancient Mariner, Part VII,*
> Samuel Taylor Coleridge (1772–1834)

IN BETWEEN SESSIONS

• This week intentionally stop for one person who you would normally "pass by." Briefly journal here (or in a separate notebook if you need more space) about your experience and share what you learned with the group.

• Rewrite the Parable of the Good Samaritan in your own context. Is there a situation at work, in your home life, or your social circle where a certain type of person is continually "passed by"? Write your own story where someone takes action and decides to be this person's neighbor.

✪ REPEAT WITH A NEW FILM OR THE SAME FILM NEXT TIME YOU MEET

THE **PARABLE** OF THE **TALENTS**

SCRIPTURE: **MATTHEW 25:14–30**
FILM: *BURIED TALENT*

♡ PRAY TOGETHER

INTRODUCTION

The Parable of the Talents is about money, or "bags of gold" as the NIV renders it. In Jesus' day, a talent was a unit of measure used to weigh precious metals and other items of value. However, the short film *Buried Talent* is about painting. So ... why isn't this film about modern-day investments? As you watch the film and explore the Scripture text, consider that the deeper meaning of the parable examines stewardship beyond finance. God leaves many things in our care: money, friendships, charity, talents, etc. The title, *Buried Talent*, is an obvious play on words. In fact, the use of the word *talent* in Western culture as a gift or skill originated with this parable! The parable also involves fear and how it can inhibit and freeze us. As you watch the film, consider the challenge the artists are given. It's an extraordinary opportunity with tremendous resources. But there's a catch ... they only have limited time and instruction.

◉ WATCH THE FILM *BURIED TALENT*

📖 READ THE PARABLE OF THE TALENTS

[14] "Again, it will be like a man going on a journey, who called his servants and entrusted his wealth to them. [15] To one he gave five bags of gold, to another two bags, and to another one bag, each according to his ability. Then he went on his journey. [16] The man who had received five bags of gold went at once and put his money to work and gained five bags more. [17] So also, the one with two bags of gold gained two more. [18] But the man who had received one bag went off, dug a hole in the ground and hid his master's money.

[19] "After a long time the master of those servants returned and settled accounts with them. [20] The man who had received five bags of gold brought the other five. 'Master,' he said, 'you entrusted me with five bags of gold. See, I have gained five more.'

[21] "His master replied, 'Well done, good and faithful servant! You have been faithful with a few things; I will put you in charge of many things. Come and share your master's happiness!'

[22] "The man with two bags of gold also came. 'Master,' he said, 'you entrusted me with two bags of gold; see, I have gained two more.'

[23] "His master replied, 'Well done, good and faithful servant! You have been faithful with a few things; I will put you in charge of many things. Come and share your master's happiness!'

[24] "Then the man who had received one bag of gold came. 'Master,' he said, 'I knew that you are a hard man, harvesting where you have not sown and gathering where you have not scattered seed. [25] So I was afraid and went out and hid your gold in the ground. See, here is what belongs to you.'

[26] "His master replied, 'You wicked, lazy servant! So you knew that I harvest where I have not sown and gather where I have not scattered seed? [27] Well then, you should have put my money on deposit with the bankers, so that when I returned I would have received it back with interest.

[28] "'So take the bag of gold from him and give it to the one who has ten bags. [29] For whoever has will be given more, and they will have an abundance. Whoever does not have, even what they have will be taken from them. [30] And throw that worthless servant outside, into the darkness, where there will be weeping and gnashing of teeth.'"

Matthew 25:14–30

CULTURAL BACKGROUND

Wealthy landowners usually delegated control and multiplication of their wealth to trained accountants or, as in the case of Jesus' parable, servants. These landowners also often embarked on long journeys. Given the time period, the value of a talent was about six thousand denarii. One denarius was a day's wage. A single talent was worth twenty years of work! The servant who received five talents was entrusted with the equivalent of a hundred years' wages!

In those days, and it still holds true today, one of the *safest* and *least profitable* ways of protecting one's money was to bury it in the ground. Such ancient buried reserves are still occasionally found to this day. This servant was afraid to do anything with his master's assets other than keep them "safely" below ground. He should've known better; the smallest possible investment—providing interest on a savings deposit—wouldn't have endangered the money and provided at least a little return.

Not only that, the principle that integrity in smaller matters qualified one to prove one's integrity in larger matters was often invoked in antiquity. It's reasonable to assume the third servant in Jesus' parable would have known how easily he could double his money and that his master was testing him. Nonetheless, the servant decided to bury his master's talent because, as he states when brought to account, "I was afraid . . . ."

⌕ DISCUSS THE FILM AND ORIGINAL PARABLE

1. How can we compare the two propositions? (investing coins in the original parable and creating art in *Buried Talent*)

2. What are some things in your life that have been entrusted to your care?

3. Do you sometimes feel that God asks much of you, but you sense a heavy burden to work it out on your own?

4. Tom's character is the most professional of the group. He has a portfolio of work and is quite organized. Given this opportunity to be free to paint whatever he likes, he freezes and fails. Can you think of a time when you froze in the face of a similar opportunity and ended up "burying" your talent? What did you learn from that situation?

5. Jamie's character is right out of college, and this is her first interview for a painting job. She's the most nervous of the group, and yet she produces a marvelous painting. Can you think of a time when you let your talent rise to the surface in spite of your fears? What did you learn from that situation?

BEHIND THE SCENES

We'd been shooting all day under the hot sun in Clovis, California, and the very last thing we had left to shoot was the scene when the wife sees the paintings for the first time. I was operating the camera, watching the scene unfold, and suddenly my eyes filled with tears. The viewfinder just went fuzzy. The scene played out, but I didn't really get to see it. I was caught up in the moment, the sheer delight the wife took in the paintings her husband had created for her and his joy in seeing her so fulfilled! The whole scene was such a powerful image of the day when the Father will turn to many and say, "Well done, good and faithful servant! Come and share in your master's happiness!"

CLOSING THOUGHTS

We are all entrusted with the talents we need to do the things God has intended for us to accomplish. This theme runs throughout Scripture. Long before Jesus' time, God entrusted two men with the talent they needed to accomplish the daunting task of constructing his tabernacle. Their names were Bezalel and Oholiab and you can read about them in Exodus 31:1–7. A few hundred years later, King Cyrus of Persia sent some Jews back to Jerusalem to rebuild the temple and wrote a decree that reads much like the commission of Bezalel and Oholiab (Ezra 1:1–2). This passage and the one in Exodus both reveal that God had certain people in certain places to accomplish certain things, and he made sure they were equipped with the talent they needed to do it! He gives people the talent they need to engage in the crafts he has set before them. God has always been moving people and equipping them to use their talents.

Now if it were only that simple.

It is interesting to note that in Jesus' day a "talent" was equivalent to twenty years worth of daily wages. We're all born with certain talents, but it takes many years to truly master them. The time we spend using our talent gives us invaluable experience. Unfortunately, many of our talents lay dormant. If we never begin, we'll never accumulate the experience we need to use our talent with the ease, gusto, and sheer enjoyment Diego does in the film! Like Bezalel, Oholiab, the painters in *Buried Talent*, and the servants in Jesus' parable, we are all charged to use the talents entrusted to us.

> When I consider how my light is spent
> Ere half my days, in this dark world and wide,
> And that one talent, which is death to hide,
> Lodged with me useless, though my soul more bent
> To serve therewith my Maker, and present
> My true account, lest he returning chide
>
> From *On His Blindness*, John Milton (1608–1674)

IN BETWEEN SESSIONS

• Take a personal talent inventory. This week keep a journal of all the things you think of that you've always wanted to do. Maybe you've always wanted to speak German, write a song, or take dance lessons. Make a list of whatever you think of and share it with the group. If two or more of you have listed the same thing, make a plan to start developing that talent. Even if you're the only one with a certain idea—puppetry or coaching T-ball, for example—find someone else in your group who will keep you accountable to take the first step.

• Take on the Rich Man's assignment! Whether you use a camera, pencil, pen, collage, or paint, create an image before your group meets. The only restriction, you have to use the color gold prominently in your work!

⌖ REPEAT WITH A NEW FILM OR THE SAME FILM NEXT TIME YOU MEET

THE **PARABLE** OF THE **LOST COIN**

SCRIPTURE: **LUKE 15:8–10**
FILM: *FOUND*

♡ PRAY TOGETHER

INTRODUCTION

Some things have low extrinsic value—such as a simple necklace given as a gift from a husband to a wife. The necklace might have cost less than one hundred dollars. But when you factor in the intrinsic value of the item—what it represents to its owner—its value is far greater, perhaps incalculable.

In the film *Kingdom of Heaven*, directed by Ridley Scott, a fictional encounter takes place between the hero of the film, Balian of Ibelin (played by Orlando Bloom), and the General Saladin (played by Ghasson Massoud). After Balian surrenders Jerusalem to Saladin he asks, "What is Jerusalem worth?" As he is walking away, Saladin dismissively states, "Nothing." Then, after a couple more steps, Saladin stops, turns to Balian, lifts both fists up in front of his chest, and says, "Everything."

The Parable of the Lost Coin is all about value. What something, or someone, is worth is completely dependent on whom you're asking.

👁 WATCH THE FILM *FOUND*

📖 READ THE PARABLE OF THE LOST COIN

[8] "Or suppose a woman has ten silver coins and loses one. Doesn't she light a lamp, sweep the house and search carefully until she finds it? [9] And when she finds it, she calls her friends and neighbors together and says, 'Rejoice with me; I have found my lost coin.' [10] In the same way, I tell you, there is rejoicing in the presence of the angels of God over one sinner who repents."

Luke 15:8–10

CULTURAL BACKGROUND

Middle Eastern history tells us that the lost coin may have been from this woman's wedding headdress, the equivalent of a modern-day wedding ring. In the first century, this coin may well have been part of a woman's dowry (the asset she brought into the marriage) — an asset of great sentimental and intrinsic value. The silver coins in her possession would likely be the only money she brings into the marriage, money that remains hers even if the marriage is dissolved. The fact that she has only ten coins (worth about ten days of a worker's wages) suggests that her father's family is not well off financially and that, if a wedding is coming, she'd be marrying into a household of equally limited means.

Floors in the ancient Middle East were often woven and therefore had a lot of cracks — many, many places where a dropped item could hide itself indefinitely. That, plus the lack of windows and bad lighting, made it nearly impossible to find something that slipped through the cracks. To locate a lost item, one had to practically turn the house upside down. Because of how much the ten coins meant to her, the woman searched diligently until she found them.

This parable of searching is one of three parables Jesus told back to back in Luke 15. It is worth noting that this parable features a female lead directly between two other parables based on the same theme with male leads. In the original Greek, the "friends and neighbors" the woman invites over to celebrate are female. In a culture that had marginalized and disenfranchised women, Jesus' day-to-day interactions and his stories emphasized the intrinsic value of women.

⌕ DISCUSS THE FILM AND ORIGINAL PARABLE

1. How does the necklace in *Found* compare to the man's other possessions?

2. If your home became engulfed in flames, and you could rescue *one* item only—the single possession that means the most to you—what item would you save?

3. If this one item were auctioned on eBay, what price do you suppose would secure the winning bid?

4. What price would you pay for it?

5. How does God value people? Why do they matter to God? What is their "intrinsic" value?

BEHIND THE SCENES

We had no money to shoot *Found*. No money, no problems ... right? The painful question we faced was, "How do we do this with so little?" Like Peter on the stormy sea, we risked stepping out on uncertain footing, not sure if we'd sink, needing Jesus to pull us out. In the end we found simple solutions to everyday production problems that didn't cost us a dime. We used a mini DV camera, a cheap tripod, a boom mic propped up against a wall (we had no operator for it), a few lights from a friend, and our key grip was a childhood friend who held a black bed sheet to block the sun. Our stand-up comedian friend, Daniel Fritz, wrote the surprisingly serious and sentimental script, acted in the film, and held a reflector board when he wasn't on camera. And with *Found* we started the practice of filming each parable short film in one day!

CLOSING THOUGHTS

In *Found* the vagabond makes his living playing an accordion on the streets for people's spare change. Then one day, while digging through a dumpster searching for his most prized possession, someone steals his accordion. Sure he found his necklace, and that was clearly very important to him. But what happens after? His accordion is gone.

A few years ago, on just another Monday, I went into work and was surprised to find out I no longer had a job. My head was spinning. Many of us have had a similar experience. Suddenly, without explanation, the thing we count on as a source of provision for our family is gone. Yes, we still have our faith, our family, and we are actively seeking a deeper, more personal relationship with Jesus ... but ... we just lost our job.

The disciples had a job to do, just like us. They were healing the sick, driving out demons, and proclaiming that the kingdom of heaven was at hand. Then one day, out of nowhere, the Pharisees grabbed the disciples' boss and crucified him. As far as they could see, their job was over. The boss was dead.

Our accordions often slip away and leave us asking, "Why?"

If you've recently lost an accordion, take heart. Jesus said, "I have told you these things, so that in me you may have peace. In this world you will have trouble. But take heart! I have overcome the world" (John 16:33).

> Amazing grace! (how sweet the sound)
> That sav'd a wretch like me!
> I once was lost, but now am found,
> Was blind, but now I see.

From the *Olney Hymns*,
John Newton (1725 – 1807)

IN BETWEEN SESSIONS

• Spend some time this week recalling a time you searched for an item that had great intrinsic value for you. It could be a wedding ring, the pocketknife your dad gave you, your great grandmother's locket, or your favorite childhood toy. Journal about your journey to recover the item. Share your story with the group the next time you meet.

- We often identify people who don't have a relationship with Jesus but begin going to church as "seekers," but in this parable God does the seeking. If we understood God's heart for people who are lost, who would you pursue that you aren't currently pursuing? List their names below. Whatever people come to mind, begin seeking them out this week. Send them a message or give them a call.

⊘ REPEAT WITH A NEW FILM OR THE SAME FILM NEXT TIME YOU MEET

THE **PARABLE** OF THE **HIDDEN TREASURE**

SCRIPTURE: **MATTHEW 13:44**
FILM: *THE MUSIC BOX*

♡ PRAY TOGETHER

INTRODUCTION

To "stumble upon something" is to find it through no effort of our own. It's an accident; in reality, that "something" finds us. Jesus says this is very similar to how the kingdom of God operates in this world. It finds us. We don't find it. This is the image Jesus paints in the Parable of the Hidden Treasure. In the short film *The Music Box*, a man is out buying antique music boxes and "stumbles upon" a box of superior value. The box played a crucial role in his childhood and has great sentimental value to him. The result is that the man will pay whatever it takes to get that box—however many zeros he must add to his check. The owners wonder if they've missed something, but they finally agree to sell. The man is ecstatic since the box is far more important to him than the money.

👁 WATCH THE FILM *THE MUSIC BOX*

📖 READ THE PARABLE OF THE HIDDEN TREASURE

⁴⁴ "The kingdom of heaven is like treasure hidden in a field. When a man found it, he hid it again, and then in his joy went and sold all he had and bought that field."

Matthew 13:44

CULTURAL BACKGROUND

First-century Palestine was an agrarian society broken up into three primary classes: those who owned land, those who leased land, and those who worked the land. Unfortunately, after paying rent, taxes, tithes, and upkeep, many of those who leased were left with very little money. The concept of having a surplus was foreign to anyone other than the elite. Modern audiences may struggle with the character in the parable selling all he had to purchase land. In our context, this would draw attention and someone else might find the treasure. However, in that day, owning land would move a person from merely being a wage laborer to having the opportunity to actually provide for his family through subsistence farming. The Greek word used for man in this parable, *anthropos*, does not necessarily imply whether this man was a landowner, tenant, or wage laborer.

It is not a stretch to imagine a story like the one Jesus tells in Matthew 13:44 being a sort of rural "urban legend" in his day and age. Many first-century farmers might have had their own anecdotal version of this story—a moment in the past when a friend literally "stumbled upon" a hidden treasure. Burying valuables in the ground was somewhat common, because banks were unusual in ancient Palestine. Farmers would often hide their treasures in their fields at secret locations. This worked well—except in cases of accidental or sudden deaths. If the farmer died unexpectedly, the secret hiding place went to the grave with him. Then, years later, a wage laborer might run his plow into an obstacle, only to find he had stumbled upon buried treasure. The laborer would sell everything he had to purchase it, knowing full well that the treasure's value would far exceed the purchase price.

○ DISCUSS THE FILM AND ORIGINAL PARABLE

1. Have you ever "stumbled upon" a great "treasure"? Explain.

2. Why do we tend to hang on to our stuff instead of exchanging it for the kingdom of God?

3. If you've already sold out to the kingdom, what benefits would you say have outweighed the costs?

4. What do you find yourself hanging onto (still) in the midst of this spiritual transaction?

5. Do you see yourself as having "stumbled upon" the kingdom, or are you more prone to see it as something you've searched for, found, and earned?

BEHIND THE SCENES

The Music Box is near and dear to our hearts for several reasons. For one, the film was shot in the director's hometown. The old man in the flashback scene is the director's father and we shot that scene in the basement he'd dug by hand thirty years ago. And the initials on the bottom of the music box are those of a friend who had departed to be with the Lord a few years back. All eighteen of the short films in this study were brought to life through the support of our friends and family. In almost every film there is something hidden—like the initials JPK—to honor those we love. This is true of almost everything anyone creates. What is important to the artist comes out in his or her artwork. If you look closely, you'll find treasures buried all around you.

CLOSING THOUGHTS

The Parable of the Hidden Treasure is found in Matthew 13, perhaps the single most illuminating chapter in the entire Bible concerning parables. In this chapter Jesus tells several parables and his disciples come right out and ask him, "Why do you speak to the people in parables?" (v. 10). His response, which has come to be known as "the Matthew Principle," goes like this: "Whoever has will be given more, and they will have an abundance. Whoever does not have, even what they have will be taken from them" (v. 12).

The brilliance of the writing in this chapter is captivating. Matthew begins with Jesus speaking in parables and his explanation of "the Matthew Principle" and ends the chapter with Jesus returning to his hometown, where he and his disciples experience "the Matthew Principle" at work. When the people of Jesus' hometown dismiss him as the carpenter's son, Jesus responds, "A prophet is not without honor except in his own town and in his own home" (v. 57) and then he departs. The very thing Jesus' hometown had—the Messiah—was taken from them. God is limitless, but we are not. Like those in Jesus' hometown, we are restricted to being in one place at one time. So when you find yourself confronted with the great value of the kingdom, like the treasure buried in the field, may you choose wisely.

But men labor under a mistake. The better part of the man is soon ploughed into the soil for compost. By a seeming fate, commonly called necessity, they are employed, as it says in an old book, laying up treasures which moth and rust will corrupt and thieves break through and steal.

Henry David Thoreau (1817–1862)

IN BETWEEN SESSIONS

• This week read Matthew 6:19–21, Matthew 10:37–39, and Mark 8:34–36 and journal your thoughts, feelings, and observations concerning what these passages have to say about what we value.

• Bury a treasure. This week "hide" something of value for someone else to find. This could be as simple as paying for someone's drink behind you in line at a coffee shop, placing an encouraging note for a loved one under their pillow, or purchasing a gift card and leaving it anonymously on the desk of someone at work who could use some help. Share what treasure you hid—and the person's reaction to finding it—with the group next time you meet.

✪ REPEAT WITH A NEW FILM OR THE SAME FILM NEXT TIME YOU MEET

THE **PARABLE** OF THE **UNMERCIFUL SERVANT**

SCRIPTURE: **MATTHEW 18:21–35**
FILM: *GNOBODY'S GNOME*

♡ PRAY TOGETHER

INTRODUCTION

We all desire to be treated mercifully. Yet, we're often merciless when put in a position to show it to others. We find ourselves torn in two. We want the bank to make an exception in our case only moments after asking for our money back at the café because they didn't prepare our drink properly. How many times have you found yourself on the phone with a customer service representative, mortgage lender, cell phone carrier, airline, or some other large institution, showing absolutely no mercy? You're listing grievances, making demands, and ultimately threatening to take your business elsewhere … unless you get your way. Then you're a few minutes late to your next meeting and expect everyone to understand. It's comical, really. At its very core, unforgiveness is patently absurd. Appropriately so, the short film adaptation of the Parable of the Unmerciful Servant is a comedy. In *Gnobody's Gnome*, a middle-aged yuppie is in deep water financially and has to get a prized garden gnome back from his neighbor in order to help pay his debts.

👁 WATCH THE FILM *GNOBODY'S GNOME*

📖 READ THE PARABLE OF THE UNMERCIFUL SERVANT

²¹ Then Peter came to Jesus and asked, "Lord, how many times shall I forgive my brother or sister who sins against me? Up to seven times?"

²² Jesus answered, "I tell you, not seven times, but seventy-seven times.

²³ "Therefore, the kingdom of heaven is like a king who wanted to settle accounts with his servants. ²⁴ As he began the settlement, a man who owed him ten thousand bags of gold was brought to him. ²⁵ Since he was not able to pay, the master ordered that he and his wife and his children and all that he had be sold to repay the debt.

²⁶ "At this the servant fell on his knees before him. 'Be patient with me,' he begged, 'and I will pay back everything.' ²⁷ The servant's master took pity on him, canceled the debt and let him go.

²⁸ "But when that servant went out, he found one of his fellow servants who owed him a hundred silver coins. He grabbed him and began to choke him. 'Pay back what you owe me!' he demanded.

²⁹ "His fellow servant fell to his knees and begged him, 'Be patient with me, and I will pay it back.'

³⁰ "But he refused. Instead, he went off and had the man thrown into prison until he could pay the debt. ³¹ When the other servants saw what had happened, they were outraged and went and told their master everything that had happened.

³² "Then the master called the servant in. 'You wicked servant,' he said, 'I canceled all that debt of yours because you begged me to. ³³ Shouldn't you have had mercy on your fellow servant just as I had on you?' ³⁴ In anger his master handed him over to the jailers to be tortured, until he should pay back all he owed.

³⁵ "This is how my heavenly Father will treat each of you unless you forgive your brother or sister from your heart."

Matthew 18:21–35

CULTURAL BACKGROUND

Jesus told the Parable of the Unmerciful Servant in response to Peter's question, "How many times shall I forgive my brother or sister who sins against me? Up to seven times?" Rabbis were known to say forgiveness was to be extended three times before finally refusing to indulge a habitual sinner. Peter believed he was being wildly magnanimous when he suggested to Jesus that people ought to be forgiven up to seven times. But Jesus instead says "seventy-seven times." This Hebrew idiom was used as an equivalent to our concept of infinity — in other words, more times than you can count.

Jesus then follows up his shocking proclamation with a parable containing a similar illusion to unlimited forgiveness. A king calls in his servants and asks them to settle accounts. One particular servant owes the king the equivalent of two hundred thousand years' wages. The figure used in the parable — ten thousand talents (bags of gold) — is similar to the phrase "seventy-seven times." The talent was the largest measure of currency in ancient Palestine, while the Greek word for ten thousand in this passage, *myrios*, was the single largest Greek numeral and also used to describe something limitless or countless. Essentially Jesus was saying the servant owed the king a debt equal to "seventy-seven times." And just like the sort of limitless forgiveness Jesus describes to Peter, the king in the parable decides to forgive the entire debt. The king is understandably enraged when he hears this same servant then choked a man who owed him one hundred denarii, a sum six-hundred thousand times smaller than a literal definition of the servant's ten thousand talent debt.

⌕ DISCUSS THE FILM AND ORIGINAL PARABLE

1. What debts are most difficult for you to forgive: the little irritations, the slaps to your ego, the ones that happen over and over, or the big deals? Why?

2. If you could see your sin from God's perspective, where would you see a pattern of repetition (doing the same wrong over and over)?

3. What about our lack of forgiveness boggles God's mind?

4. How big is your pile of IOUs before God in comparison to the pile you hold from other people?

5. How do you react to the following question: Won't being merciful to others who repeat the same sins over and over simply indulge them, giving them no reason to repent?

BEHIND THE SCENES

We had a blast creating *Gnobody's Gnome*. And we had an excellent opportunity to forgive. During the film, when Harold proclaims he wants to put in a pool, you see a shot of the backyard. What you don't see, just off frame of the shot, is an actual swimming pool. The house where we were shooting already had a swimming pool! We were rushing through the day and were all set to get the shot of the backyard, framing out the pool of course, when our production designer walked right into the middle of the shot. It was hilarious! The entire crew was inside, looking out of this big bay of windows, waiting to get this simple shot so we could go to lunch when he walked right through the shot. He looked in the windows, saw the camera and twenty people staring back at him, and froze. He was a like a deer in headlights. Then he faked left, faked right, and ran out of the shot. We all had a good laugh, got the shot, and went to lunch. Then we fired him ... just kidding!

CLOSING THOUGHTS

In his book *Kingdom, Grace, and Judgment*, Robert Farrar Capon fits all of Jesus' parables into one of those three categories. Jesus began his ministry by preaching about the kingdom of God and then shifted his emphasis to grace. As the time of the crucifixion grew near, his parables were predominately focused on judgment. Though we've adapted eighteen of Jesus' parables in *Parables Remix*, we aren't bringing all of his parables to the screen. We had to pick and choose. How did we decide which ones to adapt? Often it felt much more like the parables chose us. Something in our life happened or we were struck by a story we heard and then a light came on and we saw one of the parables in the situation. Sometimes it wasn't an event or story that inspired us but simply an object, place, or character. For instance, a garden gnome. We drew inspiration for our modern adaptations of Jesus' parables from our daily lives. When preparing his parables, Jesus must have drawn from his own life experiences in much the same way.

An eye for an eye leaves the whole world blind.

Mahatma Ghandi (1869 – 1948)

IN BETWEEN SESSIONS

• This week make a list of the people you need to forgive and why. Come prepared to discuss which grievances are easier for you to let go and which ones are more of a challenge.

• While you're creating your list of those you need to forgive, also make a list of those who have forgiven you.

⊗ REPEAT WITH A NEW FILM OR THE SAME FILM NEXT TIME YOU MEET

THE **PARABLE** OF THE **TWO DEBTORS**

SCRIPTURE: **LUKE 7:36–50**
FILM: *LIKE FATHER LIKE SON*

♡ PRAY TOGETHER

INTRODUCTION

We all have the tendency to view our sins as indicative of run-of-the-mill brokenness—and the sins of others as somehow dastardly and insidious. We may even feel entitled to the forgiveness we have experienced, like the Pharisees in Jesus' day, and begin to draw a line of demarcation between "sinners" and ourselves. Jesus tells a short parable about this penchant to lose perspective while dining at Simon the Pharisee's home. The religious leader's superior attitude toward sinners comes into sharp focus when a "sinful" woman anoints Jesus' feet at the meal. In the short film *Like Father Like Son*, a pastor cannot see the similarities between his issues and his son's issues. He is blind to his pride and hypersensitive to his son's failings. Enter the grandfather. Although he lacks physical sight, he can see clearly the parallels between his son and grandson. He sees that both are in need of forgiveness.

👁 WATCH THE FILM *LIKE FATHER LIKE SON*

📖 READ THE PARABLE OF THE TWO DEBTORS

36 When one of the Pharisees invited Jesus to have dinner with him, he went to the Pharisee's house and reclined at the table. 37 A woman in that town who lived a sinful life learned that Jesus was eating at the Pharisee's house, so she came there with an alabaster jar of perfume. 38 As she stood behind him at his feet weeping, she began to wet his feet with her tears. Then she wiped them with her hair, kissed them and poured perfume on them.

39 When the Pharisee who had invited him saw this, he said to himself, "If this man were a prophet, he would know who is touching him and what kind of woman she is—that she is a sinner."

40 Jesus answered him, "Simon, I have something to tell you."

"Tell me, teacher," he said.

41 "Two people owed money to a certain moneylender. One owed him five hundred denarii, and the other fifty. 42 Neither of them had the money to pay him back, so he forgave the debts of both. Now which of them will love him more?"

43 Simon replied, "I suppose the one who had the bigger debt forgiven."

"You have judged correctly," Jesus said.

44 Then he turned toward the woman and said to Simon, "Do you see this woman? I came into your house. You did not give me any water for my feet, but she wet my feet with her tears and wiped them with her hair. 45 You did not give me a kiss, but this woman, from the time I entered, has not stopped kissing my feet. 46 You did not put oil on my head, but she has poured perfume on my feet. 47 Therefore, I tell you, her many sins have been forgiven—as her great love has shown. But whoever has been forgiven little loves little."

48 Then Jesus said to her, "Your sins are forgiven."

49 The other guests began to say among themselves, "Who is this who even forgives sins?"

50 Jesus said to the woman, "Your faith has saved you; go in peace."

Luke 7:36–50

CULTURAL BACKGROUND

Jesus was invited to dine with a Pharisee. The culinary customs of the day required that they recline at the table, propped up by one arm, with their legs pointing away from the table, using the other arm to eat. This position would leave Jesus' feet exposed to those serving. Into this scene slipped an uninvited woman whose immorality was notorious. She may have been a prostitute, or maybe just a well-known partygoer. We don't really know what her particular sin was—except for the clear implication that her reputation preceded her. Overcome with sobbing, she knelt by Jesus' feet, showering them in her own tears and some very expensive perfume. Some have speculated that this perfume was a tool of the trade for prostitutes, while others suggest she bought this expensive ointment with the proceeds from her questionable activities. Either way, her behavior was clearly shocking to the other guests. And then, to make matters worse, she kissed Jesus' feet while trying to wipe away her tears with her unfurled hair! This was a no-no in first-century Israel. A reputable woman *never* unfurled her hair in public—which shows how blind this woman had become to others' opinions. She only cared about Jesus' opinion.

Simon the Pharisee, on the other hand, had neglected the expected etiquette for entertaining guests. He failed to provide water to wash Jesus' feet, anoint Jesus' head with oil, or greet Jesus with a kiss—such behavior is the modern-day equivalent of refusing to shake hands. It was into this sharp cultural contrast that Jesus interjected his simple yet poignant tale.

◯ DISCUSS THE FILM AND ORIGINAL PARABLE

1. When have you perceived other people wrongly, or have been wrongly perceived by others?

2. In our culture, what sins are socially "acceptable"? What sins are culturally "notorious"?

3. What actions would classify someone as a "sinful" person today?

4. How accurately do you think you see your own sinfulness?

5. Do you see your sin as bigger, smaller, or about the same as other people's sins?

BEHIND THE SCENES

Once again, we were running out of time. The sun was doing the exact same thing it did every day—slowly, steadily sinking toward the horizon. And, once again, we had only one chance to get the shot we needed. You'd think we would learn. After getting the shot of Jake pulling up to the church, we had to rush across a four-lane street to get the next one. Our camera assistant lugged the enormous camera, nearly three feet long with a 25–250mm zoom lens attached to the front, across the street like Atlas carrying the world on his shoulders. Moments later the camera was set, the white paint was ready in Jake's hands, and the director called "Action!" Jake began rolling white paint over the detailed graffiti we had commissioned for the film. A lot of time and effort went into that graffiti. And in a matter of seconds it was gone. We ran back across the street to get some close-ups and that was it; the wall, once covered with the graffiti of a rebellious son, was now white as snow. There wasn't a trace of the graffiti to be seen. Gone. Our sin is as temporary as that graffiti. Once it's covered, it's covered. Gone. That's it. White as snow. Forgiven.

CLOSING THOUGHTS

Jesus told a parable about two debtors—one owing ten times more than the other. And the moneylender forgives both debts! Then Jesus grilled Simon the Pharisee with a few well-placed questions: "Now which of them will love him more?" Simon rightly replied that the one with the bigger debt will love more. Which brought Jesus to question number two: "Do you see this woman?" This is the crux of Jesus' point, the "something" he had to tell Simon in verse 40. Sometimes we only see what we want to see and are blind to the obvious. Simon looked at this woman and could only see her sinful reputation; Jesus wanted him to see the woman's genuine response to God's limitless forgiveness. Jesus wanted Simon to see the perceived distance between his own sin and the woman's sin as truly nonexistent, that Simon's "smaller" debt was nothing to boast about—both he and the woman were sinners in God's eyes.

> Forgiving and being reconciled to our enemies or our loved ones are not about pretending that things are other than they are. It is not about patting one another on the back and turning a blind eye to the wrong. True reconciliation exposes the awfulness, the abuse, the hurt, the truth. It could even sometimes make things worse. It is a risky undertaking but in the end it is worthwhile, because in the end only an honest confrontation with reality can bring real healing. Superficial reconciliation can bring only superficial healing.
>
> Desmond Tutu (born 1931)

IN BETWEEN SESSIONS

• Take some time to think of one modern-day equivalent to the sinful woman's anointing of Jesus' feet. Journal about how you feel when you think about actually showing that sort of affection to Jesus, as if you were able to physically be with him.

• This week cut everyone a break. Pray that God would empower you with the Holy Spirit to live the words of Ephesians 4:32: "Be kind and compassionate to one another, forgiving each other, just as in Christ God forgave you." Take it easy on that person, coworker, current or former spouse, child, parent, the family member you only see at holidays, the guy who is sitting in your row on Sunday, or even yourself.

REPEAT WITH A NEW FILM OR THE SAME FILM NEXT TIME YOU MEET

THE **PARABLE** OF THE **NEW WINE** IN **OLD WINESKINS**

SCRIPTURE: **LUKE 5:33–39**
FILM: *SPILT MILK*

♡ PRAY TOGETHER

INTRODUCTION

Ecclesiastes 3:1 says, "There is a time for everything, and a season for every activity under the heavens:" Birth, death, mourning, dancing, silence, speaking … just to name a few from the list of activities mentioned there. Directly preceding the Parable of the New Wine in Old Wineskins, Jesus was questioned by the Pharisees about why his disciples didn't fast. His simple explanation, in essence, went like this: "Because I am here with them. They're celebrating now; they'll fast when I leave." The Pharisees did not see the need for "new wine" or "new wineskins" because they didn't believe Jesus was the Messiah. They didn't understand who was standing right in front of them.

The child in this film understands that milk is poured into a bowl filled with cereal. But he looks inside the fridge and sees the gallon he usually pours into the cereal and decides to use it—except that the gallon of milk is rotten. It's past its prime … and he pays a price for drinking it. Overlooking the new nonfat milk, he figures, "I can still use the gallon container because that's what I'm used to."

👁 WATCH THE FILM *SPILT MILK*

📖 READ THE PARABLE OF THE NEW WINE IN OLD WINESKINS

[33] They said to him, "John's disciples often fast and pray, and so do the disciples of the Pharisees, but yours go on eating and drinking."

[34] Jesus answered, "Can you make the friends of the bridegroom fast while he is with them? [35] But the time will come when the bridegroom will be taken from them; in those days they will fast."

[36] He told them this parable: "No one tears a piece out of a new garment to patch an old one. Otherwise, they will have torn the new garment, and the patch from the new will not match the old. [37] And no one pours new wine into old wineskins. Otherwise, the new wine will burst the skins; the wine will run out and the wineskins will be ruined. [38] No, new wine must be poured into new wineskins. [39] And no one after drinking old wine wants the new, for they say, 'The old is better.'"

Luke 5:33–39

CULTURAL BACKGROUND

The cultivation and production of wine in Israel began hundreds of years before Jesus' birth. Archaeological and written records, as well as the many Hebrew words for the various stages and types of vines, grapes, and wine, reveal that the production and consumption of wine in Jesus' time was a cultural mainstay. Wine was consumed daily, as much as one liter per person per day. Toward the end of summer, when water had been sitting in cisterns for many days, wine was added to the drinking water to improve the taste as well as kill bacteria.

Wine and wineskins were to people of the first century just as convenience store paper cups and diet soda are to us. We all know you can refill an old paper cup with new soda for less money than buying a new one filled with new soda. The problem is, after a while a reused paper cup begins to fall apart. So we throw it out and start all over again. The same was true for wine and wineskins. When you got a new batch of wine, it was no big deal to fill up your old wineskin with it—that is, until it sprang a leak (as old wineskins were prone to do). Folks wouldn't hang on to the deteriorating container and declare, "I don't care if the wine spills or not—I'm keeping my vintage wineskin!" That would be foolishness. Yet that's exactly what religious people have done and continue to do, over and over again, throughout church history. Jesus saw it happening in his own day as the Pharisees tried to hold to the wineskins of their day. He wasn't telling them that their traditions and structures were bad, but rather, like old paper cups or worn-out wineskins, they no longer served their purpose because something new was happening: Immanuel, God with us.

☌ DISCUSS THE FILM AND THE ORIGINAL PARABLE

1. What "old wineskins" do we hang on to in church today?

2. What pioneers were once "new wineskins" but are now old hat?

3. Can you think of a time that the church has responded to a new idea with, "We've never done it that way before"—and then ended up doing things the same old way?

4. What way of knowing God do you hang on to because you like (or are most comfortable with) your old cup?

5. Where do you see leaks in the church's current way of operating?

BEHIND THE SCENES

The little boy in *Spilt Milk* was a human firecracker. We could hardly keep our eyes on him, even with his mother and a teacher on set in addition to the crew. Constantly on the move, he had energy to burn and was full of enthusiasm and ideas. We'd get everything in place to do a take and he'd overfill the bowl or forget to close the fridge door. We were there to work, had our processes in place, and he was ... well ... acting like a child!

Jesus tells us we need to be like little children to enter his kingdom (Matthew 18:3). Children, like the boy in our film, are inspired by new experience, ever curious and energized by the uncertain process of exploration and discovery. They love to go on adventures and imagine new worlds. To a child, the prospect of anything "new" is exciting! When we finally called "Wrap!" and sent the boy home with his mother, we were certainly relieved. Sure, he wore us all out, was unpredictable, and wouldn't sit still — but he also gave a good performance and reminded all of us just what becoming like "little children" might mean.

CLOSING THOUGHTS

Jesus did religion differently than the Jewish leaders were used to. He "ate with sinners." He taught on hillsides and from the bows of boats. He didn't follow the "old wineskin" habits of hand washing and Sabbath keeping. As a result, the religious authorities despised Jesus. They said, in essence, "We've never done it that way before, so you're sinning." In this simple parable Jesus at once unnerved and reassured them. He wanted them to know that the old "traditions" were being tossed out like nasty old cups or leaky wineskins because they no longer did the job of holding the new wine of the gospel. Any wine connoisseur knows that wine is alive—it breathes, it expands. Jesus taught that God's Word is also alive and cannot be contained by any "once and for all" wineskin. It crosses cultures and ethnicities, and in each situation the wineskin looks different, but it's still the same old (new) wine! The skin (its container) will change, but the wine remains the same. We struggle with this today. When we find a way of doing church that works, we hang on for dear life ... sometimes years after it starts leaking. We must remember that any single wineskin cannot contain the gospel; it will always burst.

Change in all things is sweet.

From *Nicomachean Ethics*,
Aristotle (384 – 322 BC)

IN BETWEEN SESSIONS

• This week come up with another modern-day equivalent of the "new wine in old wineskins" to share with the group the next time you meet.

- Try the "new wine"! Think of something you don't normally do as part of your spiritual disciplines. Maybe you really like Bible study but aren't crazy about prayer. Maybe you enjoy meeting in a one-on-one discipleship group but have never cranked up a praise song and sang to the Lord in the privacy of your home ... or car! At least once this week, substitute a new expression of your faith for what you normally do and then journal about your experience.

⊘ REPEAT WITH A NEW FILM OR THE SAME FILM NEXT TIME YOU MEET

THE **PARABLE** OF THE **RICH FOOL**

SCRIPTURE: **LUKE 12:13–21**
FILM: *A FEW WEEKS LATER*

♡ PRAY TOGETHER

INTRODUCTION

Albert and Hazel lived next door to my parents on Cleveland Street in Kansas City, Missouri. Albert and Hazel were people of modest means living in a 1950s era one-level house in a neighborhood of 1950s era one-level houses. When Hazel died, she left behind a lot of stuff. She had closets full of brand new clothes and the trunk of her car was crammed with merchandise. No one, including her husband, imagined that Hazel was a compulsive spender, addicted to shopping. So, what did Albert do with it all? He gave it away. The short film *A Few Weeks Later*, based on this true story, takes place *after* the death of the rich fool from Jesus' original parable. The wife in the short film is the "rich fool." During her life she acquired an immense amount of clothing that she never wore. Blouses, skirts, pants, accessories— tags still attached. Now that she has died, her grieving husband must "empty the barns," so to speak, and process the parable vicariously.

👁 WATCH THE FILM *A FEW WEEKS LATER*

📖 READ THE PARABLE OF THE RICH FOOL

[16] And he told them this parable: "The ground of a certain rich man yielded an abundant harvest. [17] He thought to himself, 'What shall I do? I have no place to store my crops.'

[18] "Then he said, 'This is what I'll do. I will tear down my barns and build bigger ones, and there I will store my surplus grain. [19] And I'll say to myself, "You have plenty of grain laid up for many years. Take life easy; eat, drink and be merry."'

[20] "But God said to him, 'You fool! This very night your life will be demanded from you. Then who will get what you have prepared for yourself?'

[21] "This is how it will be with whoever stores up things for themselves but is not rich toward God."

Luke 12:16–21

CULTURAL BACKGROUND

Jesus tells this parable in response to a dispute between two brothers. Jewish law said that the eldest brother received a double share of the father's inheritance, while the rest of the money was split between the remaining brothers. We don't really know for sure, but it might be a case where a younger brother feels ripped off because of the inheritance division, so he's hoping Jesus will publicly side with him. From Jesus' perspective, this guy is trying to make this a "fairness" issue when in reality it's about greed — the desire for more stuff.

The Epicureans had a well-known philosophy in Jesus' day: "Eat, drink, and be merry." The rich man in the parable has stored up enough to do just that for many years. What he doesn't know is that his time is up. Jesus doesn't say how he died that night, only that it was the end of his road. All he'd stored up was for naught because he was forever separated from it. That is the problem with Epicureanism — you can play as much as you want, but you never know when the sand will run out of the hourglass … and then you'll need something more enduring than possessing the most toys. The question of this parable is, "How then shall we live?" Jesus' answer: "Be rich toward God." Spend more time and energy acquiring wisdom from God than accumulating "stuff." Live your life as though tomorrow may indeed be your final day.

◯ DISCUSS THE FILM AND THE ORIGINAL PARABLE

1. How do we know when we have "enough"?

2. What would change in your life if you stopped acquiring things once you really had "enough"?

3. What percentage of your stuff could you throw away before you'd start missing it?

4. What would change for you if you knew your hourglass would run out tomorrow?

5. What would it look like to be "rich toward God"?

BEHIND THE SCENES

At first, developing scripts for our films was incredibly frustrating. We would read a parable and analyze it sequentially. This happened, then that happened, etc. We'd try to come up with a modern setting or character for the parable and get stuck. When we reached a dead end, we stopped looking at the parable and started talking about life. We couldn't see the forest for the trees until we started sharing stories we had heard or read such as Albert and Hazel's. Hazel's compulsion led her to try to have it all. Then she died. Albert, with the help of his neighbor (my mom), was left to account for all of Hazel's possessions and send them off to charity. Suddenly we saw the connection to the rich fool, which became the basis for the film *A Few Weeks Later*. My mom and I developed the script, and a few months later we were shooting the film.

CLOSING THOUGHTS

The following are excerpts from the *Parables Remix* newsletter dated November 23, 2006:

> Some of you may have known Dean Ramsey. He died last week. I can remember having dinner with him, spending time with him, and talking with him last Christmas in Dodge City, Kansas. Over the years, Dean and his wife, Glenna, have sent my brothers and me Christmas ornaments every single year. They were friends of my maternal grandparents, and through them friends with our entire family. I spent time in their home in Southern California when I lived out there. Death is a part of life, as we all know. This year I know I won't be getting a Christmas ornament from Dean Ramsey. Yet I am thankful for all the years he sent me an ornament. I have those gifts of love he gave me as a testimony to the love he had for those in his life. None of us know the day or hour we will meet the end of our existence in this mortal coil. What will happen to everything we have done and collected at that point? This question is part of Jesus' Parable of the Rich Fool ...
>
> "But God said to him, 'You fool! This very night your life will be demanded from you. Then who will get what you have prepared for yourself? This is how it will be with anyone who stores up things for himself but is not rich toward God" (Luke 12:20–21).
>
> How can we be rich toward God?
>
> "Command those who are rich in this present world not to be arrogant nor to put their hope in wealth, which is so

uncertain, but to put their hope in God, who richly provides us with everything for our enjoyment. Command them to do good, to be rich in good deeds, and to be generous and willing to share. In this way they will lay up treasure for themselves as a firm foundation for the coming age, so that they may take hold of the life that is truly life" (1 Timothy 6:17–19).

Dean Ramsey shared; he was generous; he was rich toward God. Yes, all he ever gave me was a Christmas ornament every year. Yes, I am calling that a good deed. Because a gift of love, no matter how small, is always a treasure.

> Money never made a man happy yet, nor will it. There is nothing in its nature to produce happiness. The more a man has, the more he wants. Instead of its filling a vacuum, it makes one. If it satisfies one want, it doubles and trebles that want another way. That was a true proverb of the wise man, rely upon it: "Better is little with the fear of the Lord, than great treasure, and trouble therewith."
>
> From *Old Jonathan's Jottings; or,*
> *Light and Lessons from Daily Life*,
> David Alfred Doudney (1811–1893)

IN BETWEEN SESSIONS

• This week take time to write your own eulogy. What do you want said about you when you're gone?

• "Empty your barns." Go through your wallet—do you have gift cards you haven't used? Pool them together and give them to those in need. Empty out those closets or shelves that hold your excess and give away what you don't need.

⊘ REPEAT WITH A NEW FILM OR THE SAME FILM NEXT TIME YOU MEET

THE **PARABLE** OF THE **TWO SONS**

SCRIPTURE: **MATTHEW 21:28–32**
FILM: *BEYOND BEAUTIFUL*

♡ PRAY TOGETHER

INTRODUCTION

After hearing the Parable of the Two Sons, Jesus' listeners judged as obedient the son who *said he would not go* work in his father's vineyard, but later *did go*. God wants all of us to work in the vineyard, whether we say we're going to or not. In John 15:5, Jesus puts it another way, "I am the vine; you are the branches. If you remain in me and I in you, you will bear much fruit; apart from me you can do nothing." In the short film *Beyond Beautiful*, the work that has to be done—going on a blind date—is really only the beginning of a budding romantic relationship between two of the characters. In the same way, the reward for choosing to do the work in our Father's vineyard is a deep and abiding relationship with God . . . the best kind of romance.

◉ WATCH THE FILM *BEYOND BEAUTIFUL*

📖 READ THE PARABLE OF THE TWO SONS

28 "What do you think? There was a man who had two sons. He went to the first and said, 'Son, go and work today in the vineyard.'

29 " 'I will not,' he answered, but later he changed his mind and went.

30 "Then the father went to the other son and said the same thing. He answered, 'I will, sir,' but he did not go.

31 "Which of the two did what his father wanted?"

"The first," they answered.

Jesus said to them, "Truly I tell you, the tax collectors and the prostitutes are entering the kingdom of God ahead of you. 32 For John came to you to show you the way of righteousness, and you did not believe him, but the tax collectors and the prostitutes did. And even after you saw this, you did not repent and believe him."

Matthew 21:28–32

CULTURAL BACKGROUND

Immediately following Jesus' triumphant entry into Jerusalem, his driving out of those who were buying and selling in the temple courts, his healing of the blind and lame there, and his cursing a fruitless fig tree outside the city, the chief priests and elders of the people demanded to know by whose authority Jesus did all these things. In response, Jesus first chose the direct approach: "I will also ask you one question. If you answer me, I will tell you by what authority I am doing these things. John's baptism—where did it come from? Was it from heaven, or of human origin?"(Matthew 21:24–25). Those questioning him were stuck, and they knew it.

Jesus then went on to tell the first in a series of three parables about obedience. He wanted to highlight the difference between those who talk a big faith game and don't really mean it and those whose actions speak louder than their words. Jesus' critics pilloried him for neglecting the big shots in the synagogue and befriending tax collectors and prostitutes. But Jesus wanted them to know that God isn't impressed by big talk. In one sense, it is so simple: showing up is all it takes to impress God. Simple, but not easy. God can wait until day's end to determine if a person is sincere. When Jesus proclaimed the arrival of the kingdom of God, the scribes and Pharisees (who were zealous for its arrival) were no-shows! Hookers and swindlers, on the other hand, made a beeline for the offer of Jesus' grace.

DISCUSS THE FILM AND THE ORIGINAL PARABLE

1. Will the kingdom of God be populated with "church folk" or with "ruffians"?

2. With what standard will God judge us at the end of the day?

3. For what task does the Father want us to show up?

4. In his epistle James writes, "Faith by itself, if it is not accompanied by action, is dead" (James 2:17). How do you balance faith and works?

5. How is the statement, "I will show you my faith by what I do," different than the concept of salvation by works?

BEHIND THE SCENES

The final shot in *Beyond Beautiful* is one of my favorite moments in all eighteen of the *Parables Remix* short films. Not only is it the last shot in the film, it was also the last shot of the day (called the "martini shot" on a film set!). We'd worked diligently all day to bring another parable to the screen and now we were almost done. In the scene, characters Charlie and Emma walk down a path together as the focus gently fades, the colored lanterns suspended above the court-yard becoming soft orbs of light. There is something special in the image, the simplicity of it, and how it somehow represents the entire emotion of the story.

Finding our place in the kingdom, where we will bear fruit, is like walking down a path, hand in hand with Jesus. There will be times of pruning, of course, and obedience is not always easy, but it is simple. When we are obedient to walk hand in hand with Jesus, down the path in the vineyard he has called us to, things will become softer, lighter, and more beautiful. Beyond beautiful.

CLOSING THOUGHTS

Earlier in Matthew 21, the fig tree Jesus cursed was covered in leaves, but had no fruit. This is out of the ordinary. If a fig tree is covered in leaves, that is a sign it has borne fruit. Jesus came across a fig tree that "appeared" to be fruitful, but in fact it was barren.

The following is from a monologue I wrote and performed enti-tled *Faith* (the mini-movie is available for purchase at WorshipHouse Media.com):

> Does it take faith to believe my grandfather is in heaven now, even though I saw his body in a casket being lowered in the ground? I know he's not here anymore. And I believe he's in heaven. But what do I do with that?
>
> There's this story my grandfather used to tell, that his grandfather told him. My great-great-grandfather's parents took him to see the French tightrope walker, the Great Blon-din, walk across Niagara Falls on a tightrope. He made it across the falls, and everyone cheered. Then he walked across with a wheelbarrow full of potatoes and everybody went crazy.

He did that a couple more times; then he asked the crowd if they believed he could walk across the tightrope with a person in the wheelbarrow. They said they did. Then he asked for a volunteer. Supposedly, my great-great-grandfather's hand shot up in the air and his little voice belted out, "Me, me, pick me!" His parents hushed him up and everyone let out a nervous laugh. The faith of a child diffused the tension and Blondin went on with the show. Was that faith?

Because cigarette smoking causes cancer, my grandfather's body is six feet underground right now. That's my wheelbarrow full of potatoes. Do I believe cigarettes might give me cancer? Sure I do. I believe it. Like the devil believes in God. Now faith is confidence in what we hope for and assurance about what we do not see. So what's not faith? Another part of the Bible says faith without works is dead. If you just believe but don't do anything with that belief, that's NOT faith. Faith without works … in other words, belief without action … is dead faith. Faith without works is dead. The more I think about it, I'd like to rephrase that a bit. I'd like to say faith without works is belief.

Faith without works is belief.

I believe cigarettes might give me cancer. But if I had faith, I'd quit.

Well done is better than well said.

Benjamin Franklin (1706–1790)

IN BETWEEN SESSIONS

- This week read Matthew 21:1–22:14 at least three times. There is so much layered into all that happens in those sixty verses. Write down your observations, thoughts, and feelings and come prepared to share them with the group next time you meet.

- "Work it out." If there is something you've felt you'd like to do — volunteer at a homeless shelter, teach in the children's ministry, engage in street evangelism, invite someone to church, fast, spend more time in intercessory prayer, or help with the janitorial work at the church — do it. Faith without works is dead.

ⓦ REPEAT WITH A NEW FILM OR THE SAME FILM NEXT TIME YOU MEET

THE **PARABLE** OF THE **GOOD SHEPHERD**

SCRIPTURE: **JOHN 10:11–18**
FILM: *THE GOOD SHEPHERD*

♡ PRAY TOGETHER

INTRODUCTION

Love always shows itself through a willingness to sacrifice for the beloved. Jesus spent a lot of time and energy expressing his love through his words and actions long before his ultimate sacrifice on the cross. His opponents cared little for Jesus' good intentions, or for that matter the object of his affections; they were rule followers and sought to take his life for claiming to be God. In the short film *The Good Shepherd*, a little girl desperately wants to care for the hamsters from her older sister's class (on loan from school). Her snooty older sister isn't really concerned with the welfare of the animals — she sees them more as a badge of prestige than creatures worthy of her nurture. This creates a crisis in the younger sister, a committed animal lover. If she tries to help the hamsters, she knows her sister will rat her out (no pun intended) for an accident that she caused earlier in the day. Love, however, wins out, as the younger sister sacrifices herself in order to make sure that the pets have been properly fed and watered.

👁 WATCH THE FILM *THE GOOD SHEPHERD*

📖 READ THE PARABLE OF THE GOOD SHEPHERD

[11] "I am the good shepherd. The good shepherd lays down his life for the sheep. [12] The hired hand is not the shepherd and does not own the sheep. So when he sees the wolf coming, he abandons the sheep and runs away. Then the wolf attacks the flock and scatters it. [13] The man runs away because he is a hired hand and cares nothing for the sheep.

[14] "I am the good shepherd; I know my sheep and my sheep know me— [15] just as the Father knows me and I know the Father—and I lay down my life for the sheep. [16] I have other sheep that are not of this sheep pen. I must bring them also. They too will listen to my voice, and there shall be one flock and one shepherd. [17] The reason my Father loves me is that I lay down my life—only to take it up again. [18] No one takes it from me, but I lay it down of my own accord. I have authority to lay it down and authority to take it up again. This command I received from my Father."

John 10:11 – 18

CULTURAL BACKGROUND

Some cultures herd sheep with dogs and whistles. They drive the sheep where they want them to go. This was not true for Jewish shepherds. They led and protected the sheep. The sheep became trusting of their shepherd (if he was good), following the sound of his voice. This is love-based shepherding, not fear-based shepherding. Notice how Peter caught on to this model in 1 Peter 5:2 – 4: "Be shepherds of God's flock that is under your care, watching over them—not because you must, but because you are willing, as God wants you to be; not pursuing dishonest gain, but eager to serve; not lording it over those entrusted to you, but being examples to the flock. And when the Chief Shepherd appears, you will receive the crown of glory that will never fade away."

Jesus makes a clear distinction between the good shepherd and the "hired hand." Most of the time they look about the same ... until the wolf comes. Then the difference is apparent. The hired hand runs—no sense in sacrificing for some dumb sheep. The good shepherd stands his ground. He's willing to take a hit for the sheep because it's not just a job for the good shepherd—he actually loves the sheep.

Jesus goes on to say that he is that good shepherd for us. Jesus cares about his sheep (us) so much that he was willing to lay down his life (on the cross) to stop the wolf from devouring us.

○ DISCUSS THE FILM AND THE ORIGINAL PARABLE

1. What things in your life are you willing to sacrifice for?

2. How does this parable change or add to your understanding of Jesus' sacrifice on the cross for you?

3. How can we tell the difference between the shepherd's voice and other voices?

4. Did you view religion as fear-based or love-based when you were growing up?

5. What are some examples of "hired hand" leaders today? What distinguishes "good shepherds" from these "hired hands"?

BEHIND THE SCENES

The post-production of any film includes a process referred to as "color correction." During this step, all the assembled images of the final film must be "corrected" so they work together as a visual whole. A filmmaker can do many things to alter the original image, such as increase or decrease contrast, adjust the appearance of skin tones, or add an overall tint to the picture. With *The Good Shepherd* we decided to give the entire film a tint, similar to the popular film *Amélie* (2001, directed by Jean-Pierre Jeunet). We were looking at a perfectly calibrated monitor in a high-end Hollywood color suite when we made the decision. Unfortunately, many people view the film imperfectly calibrated in an uncontrolled environment. Very few see it as it was intended.

Two thousand years ago, Jesus attempted to communicate with people to help them understand why he was on earth. But they didn't hear what he so desperately wanted them to hear. Instead, they heard blasphemy and decided to kill him. Of course, that gave Jesus the very opportunity to lay down his life for all.

CLOSING THOUGHTS

A few years back a friend of mine pulled up stakes in suburbia, shut down his company to work for a non-profit, and moved his wife and new baby girl to a low-income area near downtown Kansas City, Kansas. He told me how he and his wife viewed this decision as a sacrifice, opting to ratchet down their lifestyle and move to a part of town where not everyone looked like them or even spoke English — all in order to put flesh and blood on the Great Commission. What they have been surprised by is how much they are enjoying the sacrifice.

This caused me to reexamine the passage in Philippians 2 regarding Jesus Christ's humanity with one simple question in mind: Did Jesus enjoy living?

> In your relationships with one another, have the same mindset as Christ Jesus: Who, being in very nature God, did not consider equality with God something to be used to his own advantage; rather, he made himself nothing by taking the very nature of a servant, being made in human likeness. And being found in

appearance as a man, he humbled himself by becoming obedient to death—even death on a cross! (Philippians 2:5–8)

If you carefully read these verses, you see the emphasis of humility is on Jesus' obedience to death. Of course he had to be human in order to die. It is too simple to turn him into a heroic Spartan-like character who lived his entire life dedicated to his gruesome death. Perhaps he enjoyed living so much that his cry, "My Father, if it is not possible for this cup to be taken away unless I drink it, may your will be done"(Matthew 26:42), was not merely because he did not want to experience the great pain coming his way, but that he truly did not want to die.

O Jesus, meek and humble of heart, hear me.

From the desire of being esteemed, deliver me, Jesus.
From the desire of being loved, deliver me, Jesus.
From the desire of being extolled, deliver me, Jesus.
From the desire of being honored, deliver me, Jesus.
From the desire of being praised, deliver me, Jesus.
From the desire of being preferred to others, deliver me, Jesus.
From the desire of being consulted, deliver me, Jesus.
From the desire of being approved, deliver me, Jesus.
From the fear of being humiliated, deliver me, Jesus.
From the fear of being despised, deliver me, Jesus.
From the fear of suffering rebukes, deliver me, Jesus.
From the fear of being calumniated, deliver me, Jesus.
From the fear of being forgotten, deliver me, Jesus.
From the fear of being ridiculed, deliver me, Jesus.
From the fear of being wronged, deliver me, Jesus.
From the fear of being suspected, deliver me, Jesus.

That others may be loved more than I,
Jesus, grant me the grace to desire it.
That others may be esteemed more than I,
Jesus, grant me the grace to desire it.
That in the opinion of the world,
others may increase, and I may decrease,
Jesus, grant me the grace to desire it.
That others may be chosen and I set aside,
Jesus, grant me the grace to desire it.

That others may be praised and I unnoticed,
Jesus, grant me the grace to desire it.
That others may be preferred to me in everything,
Jesus, grant me the grace to desire it.
That others may become holier than I,
provided that I may become as holy as I should,
Jesus, grant me the grace to desire it.

Litany of Humility,
Rafael Cardinal Merry del Val (1865 – 1930)

IN BETWEEN SESSIONS

• Read Philippians 2:1 – 11 at least three times this week. Journal your thoughts and feelings about how you could "in your relationships with one another, have the same mindset as Christ Jesus" (Philippians 2:5).

• Rewrite the Parable of the Good Shepherd in your own context, a modern-day setting that resonates with you. Who would be the sheep, the wolf, the hired hands, and the shepherd? Come prepared to share your idea with the group the next time you meet.

REPEAT WITH A NEW FILM OR THE SAME FILM NEXT TIME YOU MEET

THE **PARABLE** OF THE **BUDDING FIG TREE**

SCRIPTURE: **MATTHEW 24:32–35**
FILM: *TRACTOR SAFETY TIPS*

♡ PRAY TOGETHER

INTRODUCTION

Most of us fail to read the manual when we acquire a new toy or gadget. We want to start playing or using it immediately. In the short film *Tractor Safety Tips*, the owner of a new riding lawn mower is no exception. Because of drowsiness from not reading the warning label on his medication, he decides to skip the lawn mower instructions and misses some crucial safety warnings. The result of his irresponsible impatience is disastrous. Double vision causes him to smack his head on a tree branch. He passes out only to awaken to see his new lawn mower, now unmanned and moving of its own volition, bursting into flames as it collides with a propane tank. If only he had heeded the manual's warnings!

In an effort to race forward to the "end" (when Jesus sets up his glorious kingdom), we overlook his warnings that calamities must come first. This news, on the surface, is discouraging ... yet it heralds the great consummation of all things. Luke's gospel puts it this way: "When these things begin to take place, stand up and lift up your heads, because your redemption is drawing near" (Luke 21:28).

👁 WATCH THE FILM *TRACTOR SAFETY TIPS*

📖 READ THE PARABLE OF THE BUDDING FIG TREE

32 "Now learn this lesson from the fig tree: As soon as its twigs get tender and its leaves come out, you know that summer is near. 33 Even so, when you see all these things, you know that it is near, right at the door. 34 Truly I tell you, this generation will certainly not pass away until all these things have happened. 35 Heaven and earth will pass away, but my words will never pass away."

Matthew 24:32–35

CULTURAL BACKGROUND

In Matthew 24, Jesus gives a laundry list of warning signs (things that must happen before the end of all things). Failure to obey these warnings, according to Jesus, is akin to missing out on the obvious signs of summer. In Israel, the fig tree was well known as the most accurate barometer of summer's arrival—it withholds its blossom until the final freeze of spring has passed. Any farmer worth his salt knew that you couldn't reliably proceed with the business of summer until the fig tree signaled the season's arrival.

In the same way Jesus warned his followers that calamities such as false messiahs (vv. 4–5), wars and rumors of wars (v. 6), famines and earthquakes (v. 7), and persecution (vv. 9–10) might cause anxiety in unobservant disciples. Jesus wanted those who fear the destruction of winter to see such calamities as fig tree-like signs that summer (i.e., the end of time and the establishment of God's kingdom) is imminent. It is probable that some of those who heard Jesus' warnings recorded in Matthew 24 lived to see the destruction of Jerusalem and the temple in 70 AD by the future Roman emperor, Titus. They may have recalled Jesus' words in response to the great buildings of the temple and their certain demise: "not one stone here will be left on another" (v. 2). The temple was totally destroyed and set on fire. The Roman soldiers literally had to pry the stones of the temple apart to get the melted gold from between them.

◯ DISCUSS THE FILM AND THE ORIGINAL PARABLE

1. Why are we so prone to skip instructions?

2. Have you ever experienced disaster because you failed to read or follow the instructions?

3. Why does Jesus use the fig tree as his object lesson in this parable?

4. What happens to believers who fail to discern the "signs"?

5. In what ways do we get caught off guard by or even caught up in current events?

BEHIND THE SCENES

Like the treasures of the temple sacked by the Romans in 70 AD, the original version of *Tractor Safety Tips* has been lost to history. The script we shot included the title character owning a cute little white dog. You can probably guess what happened to the cuddly canine— and why we wisely decided to reshoot (hey, we're animal lovers!). In the version of the film you watched, the man looks in shock as his lawn mower strikes a propane tank and explodes. (Aside: The shed and the propane tank were not actually there, but digitally inserted later.) But the original scene also included the sound of a barking dog followed by white puffballs shooting out the side of the runaway tractor. We actually shot the mower driving over pillow stuffing to get the effect and had to rig the mower to run with no one on it by weighing down the seat. We also ran a rope around a tree and had another vehicle towing the mower.

CLOSING THOUGHTS

Amid Jesus' warnings of the destruction of the temple and the eventual end of the world as we know it, he slips in an incredibly encouraging statement: "Heaven and earth will pass away, but my words will never pass away" (v. 35). In fifty years, will they call the first part of the twenty-first century the beginning of the second Great Depression, just another recession, or something else entirely? With the perspective of history, we will look back on these days and have a better idea of what exactly was happening all around us. Though we are eternal beings, created in God's image and designed to be with him forever, we are metaphysically marooned in the present—caught in the stream of the here and now. The world is much clearer in the rearview mirror than through the windshield. We don't know for certain what will happen tonight let alone next year. Only God has the power to share information about the future with us. Despite the dire warnings found in Matthew 24, and in the spirit of the comfort found in verse 35, God's most consistent message to mankind has been peace.

> "For to us a child is born, to us a son is given, and the government will be on his shoulders. And he will be called Wonderful Counselor, Mighty God, Everlasting Father, Prince of Peace." (Isaiah 9:6)

> "I have told you these things, so that in me you may have peace. In this world you will have trouble. But take heart! I have overcome the world." (John 16:33)

Do you see the trend? When God tells us about the future, he gives us peace. Being human means not knowing what is going to happen next, and yet the message from God himself concerning the future is steady and simple. Peace.

> O, that a man might know
> The end of this day's business ere it come!
> *Julius Caesar*, Act 5, Scene 1,
> William Shakespeare (1564–1616)

IN BETWEEN SESSIONS

• This week read Matthew 24 in its entirety at least three times. Journal your thoughts and feelings about Jesus' warnings of what to expect in the days to come.

• Write down a prediction for the next year. At the start of the next meeting, have one of the group members record each prediction "for posterity." Then, twelve months from now, revisit the list to see if anyone's predictions came true. (Have fun with this one!)

⌗ REPEAT WITH A NEW FILM OR THE SAME FILM NEXT TIME YOU MEET

THE **PARABLE** OF THE **RICH MAN** AND **LAZARUS**

SCRIPTURE: **LUKE 16:19–31**
FILM: *AFTERLIFE*

♡ PRAY TOGETHER

INTRODUCTION

In the film *Afterlife*, Mary has had an automobile accident that leads to a near-death experience in which she perceives hell as a vivid reality. When she wakes up in a hospital, her sister, who also happens to be a minister, tries to convince her that hell isn't real and that her experience is easily explained away. This "explaining away" has always been a temptation, since many feel that a "loving God" could never punish people.

In this parable, Jesus tells the story of an affluent man who cannot imagine a reversal of fortune in the afterlife. He lived in luxury on earth but finds himself on the other side in hell. Even after death, the rich man tries to pull aristocratic strings—barking out requests to Abraham that poor Lazarus function as his servant.

👁 WATCH THE FILM *AFTERLIFE*

📖 READ THE PARABLE OF THE RICH MAN AND LAZARUS

[19] "There was a rich man who was dressed in purple and fine linen and lived in luxury every day. [20] At his gate was laid a beggar named Lazarus, covered with sores [21] and longing to eat what fell from the rich man's table. Even the dogs came and licked his sores.

[22] "The time came when the beggar died and the angels carried him to Abraham's side. The rich man also died and was buried. [23] In Hades, where he was in torment, he looked up and saw Abraham far away, with Lazarus by his side. [24] So he called to him, 'Father Abraham, have pity on me and send Lazarus to dip the tip of his finger in water and cool my tongue, because I am in agony in this fire.'

[25] "But Abraham replied, 'Son, remember that in your lifetime you received your good things, while Lazarus received bad things, but now he is comforted here and you are in agony. [26] And besides all this, between us and you a great chasm has been set in place, so that those who want to go from here to you cannot, nor can anyone cross over from there to us.'

[27] "He answered, 'Then I beg you, father, send Lazarus to my family, [28] for I have five brothers. Let him warn them, so that they will not also come to this place of torment.'

[29] "Abraham replied, 'They have Moses and the Prophets; let them listen to them.'

[30] " 'No, father Abraham,' he said, 'but if someone from the dead goes to them, they will repent.'

[31] "He said to him, 'If they do not listen to Moses and the Prophets, they will not be convinced even if someone rises from the dead.' "

Luke 16:19–31

CULTURAL BACKGROUND

In Luke 16 Jesus tells two different parables featuring rich people. In the Parable of the Rich Man and Lazarus, the rich man remains nameless. All we know is that he has five brothers and wears the purple clothing of an aristocrat. In the parable he appeals to Abraham as a fellow Israelite, assuming it will somehow buy him special privilege—if not his own rescue, then at least of his siblings. Abraham tells the rich man of the harsh realities of eternity: judgment is irrevocable. In fact, there is a "chasm" between heaven and hell, and after death it cannot be crossed. We naturally may minimize the irrevocable nature of hell, but in this parable Jesus underlines its permanence. There is no chance of appeal.

The rich man was hoping to get a free pass based on his resumé; as far as he was concerned, hell wasn't on the radar screen. The point of contrast in the parable is between this man's riches and the abject poverty of Lazarus. The Scripture tells us that Lazarus was hoping for some bread scraps from this bourgeois's table, which refers to the use of bread as napkins in wealthy Middle Eastern households. The rich would wipe their hands on the bread and toss it to the floor as unfit for their consumption—and Lazarus wasn't too proud to fight the dogs for the scraps.

Note that the rich man didn't end up in hell because of sins of commission (wicked acts) but because of sins of omission (failure to see the neediness of Lazarus and respond). It's not that sins of commission don't matter; rather, Jesus points out how sinful it is to ignore suffering and pain around us.

First John 3:17 puts it this way: "If anyone has material possessions and sees a brother or sister in need but has no pity on them, how can the love of God be in that person?"

Q DISCUSS THE FILM AND THE ORIGINAL PARABLE

1. Why do we find hell to be an objectionable concept?

2. How do we try to explain it away?

3. In what ways do we rely on our heritage or our earthly accomplishments to keep us from eternal trouble? In other words, what resumé items do you believe will get you a free pass to heaven?

4. What sins of omission might God bring to our attention in eternity?

5. If we truly perceived hell as a reality, how would it change our daily behavior? Our dealings with others? Our spiritual lives?

BEHIND THE SCENES

The entire scene of Mary driving at the beginning of *Afterlife* is a perfect example of the "smoke and mirrors" in cinema. The profile shots of Mary driving were actually the actress. In the wide shots of the car driving down the road, our assistant director was behind the wheel. For the shots from directly in front of the car, where you could see the character Mary "driving," the car wasn't even moving! We rigged up a light behind the car, waved a branch in front of it to simulate motion, and had a couple crew members shake the car slightly, while the actress "drove" the car. It is fun to watch the finished sequence and know how all those little "manufactured" pieces came together to form "reality"! Unfortunately, our beliefs about the afterlife can become just as distorted when we don't anchor them to the truths presented in God's Word.

CLOSING THOUGHTS

Much discussion has surrounded the subject of hell over the centuries. Many world religions embrace the idea of eternal damnation or even annihilation for the souls of evil people. Within Christianity itself, there are wide differences of opinion: from those who believe in a literal hell, like the one described in this parable, to annihilation of the soul, to Christian universalism, the idea that all human souls eventually arrive in heaven. Even those within the same denomination—who use the exact same Bible as a starting point—often disagree whether or not hell actually exists.

In the Parable of the Rich Man and Lazarus, Jesus doesn't seem to paint a very ambiguous picture concerning the existence of hell. Whether you believe Jesus' parable should be taken more literally or more figuratively, there is no doubt about the final destinations of the rich man and Lazarus in the context of the story. Many modern theologians have arrived at the conclusion that hell, whatever or wherever it may be, is the logical ultimate destination for persons exercising their free will to reject the will of God. All of the discourse and debate surrounding the subject of hell lead one to the conclusion that the Bible is either (1) not clear enough or (2) all too clear.

Whatever we decide we believe on the subject, we can all take comfort in this clear description of our Father in heaven: "He is patient with you, not wanting anyone to perish, but everyone to come to repentance" (2 Peter 3:9).

> Through me you go to the grief wracked city;
> Through me you go to everlasting pain;
> Through me you go [to] pass among lost souls ...
> Abandon all hope—
> Ye Who Enter Here.
>
> The inscription over the Gate of Hell,
> from *The Divine Comedy: Inferno*,
> Dante Alighieri (1265–1321)

IN BETWEEN SESSIONS

• This week, using a resource such as the *Strong's Concordance*, Biblegateway.com, or a study Bible, research the subject of hell in the Bible. Before you begin your research, write down a couple sentences describing what you think you will find. Then journal your thoughts and feelings concerning how hell is actually described in the Bible.

• Throughout the next week, ask at least three people what they believe about hell. Try to get as broad a sample as possible: ask someone from work or school, a relative, a friend, or even a complete stranger. Compare their thoughts with what you discovered in your research.

⌖ **REPEAT WITH A NEW FILM OR THE SAME FILM NEXT TIME YOU MEET**

THE **PARABLE** OF THE **FRIEND** AT **MIDNIGHT**

SCRIPTURE: **LUKE 11:5–8**
FILM: *OUT OF REACH*

♡ PRAY TOGETHER

INTRODUCTION

The Parable of the Friend at Midnight explores prayer, particularly persistence in prayer. There's no better example of persistence and faith than that of a child (Luke 18:17). Jesus even tells us to have faith like a child. The children in the short film *Out of Reach* are irresistible. In fact, one can't help but wonder how the father could resist the requests of his daughter ... as she leans over his shoulder and begs him through her missing front teeth.

That's probably how God sees us ... not as annoying people pounding on the door at midnight, but as adorable children. Of course, I suppose it depends on whether you believe God is mostly mad, sad, or glad. You may view God as an angry Father who knows all about the bad things you've done and desires to punish you. You may view God as a sorrowful Father, deeply troubled by all the pain in the world. Or, you may see God as mostly glad, a Father who loves you and all his children more than they could ever imagine and is thrilled to hear from them.

◉ WATCH THE FILM *OUT OF REACH*

📖 READ THE PARABLE OF THE FRIEND AT MIDNIGHT

⁵ Then Jesus said to them, "Suppose you have a friend, and you go to him at midnight and say, 'Friend, lend me three loaves of bread; ⁶ a friend of mine on a journey has come to me, and I have no food to offer him.' ⁷ And suppose the one inside answers, 'Don't bother me. The door is already locked, and my children and I are in bed. I can't get up and give you anything.' ⁸ I tell you, even though he will not get up and give you the bread because of friendship, yet because of your shameless audacity he will surely get up and give you as much as you need."

Luke 11:5–8

CULTURAL BACKGROUND

Jesus isn't suggesting here that God is like a reluctant, sleepy neighbor; rather, he's saying that God responds to persistence. This persistence in prayer is a boldness that stays at it until God answers. Such persistence indicates faith, and God responds to faith (Hebrews 11:6). The elements of the parable would've been familiar to first-century Jews. This request of the neighbor was nothing unusual, since all communities saw hospitality as a civic obligation. The visitor (who often traveled late at night to avoid the stifling heat) was to be treated hospitably, not just by his actual hosts, but also by the entire community. The social requirement to provide food and shelter were givens, and it was probably normal to offer guests unbroken loaves of bread rather than leftover scraps. Bread was used as a utensil in Jesus' day, similar to knives and forks. Since baking was often a communal activity, the host knew at once who might have fresh, unbroken loaves available.

The assumed question of the parable is: *Can you imagine asking your neighbor for a hand in hospitality and being refused?* The implied answer is a decisive, "No way!" People in Eastern cultures would have seen "door locked" and "kids in bed" as bogus excuses, a shirking of communal responsibility. Just as they couldn't imagine a neighbor being so inhospitable, Jesus is saying we shouldn't view God as reluctant to answer our prayers. We don't need to bug God; God isn't reluctant to give us what we need. We must, however, persist in prayer so that God sees faith and rewards it.

Q DISCUSS THE FILM AND THE ORIGINAL PARABLE

1. Do you feel timid about approaching God with your requests?

2. This parable tells a story of someone pounding on a neighbor's door on behalf of someone else—a friend from out of town. How boldly do you pray for the needs of others?

3. Do you ever feel as though you're bugging God with your prayers?

4. Does it sometimes feel as though God is standing on the other side of the door telling you to go away?

5. If possible, give an example of a situation for which you prayed persistently and God answered those prayers.

BEHIND THE SCENES

The toy fire truck in *Out of Reach* actually belonged to my father when he was a child. When we were working through the story idea for *Out of Reach*, we were trying to come up with a modern scenario where the person being asked a favor would feel inclined to help—given that in the original context, the neighbor would have felt such an obligation even though it was the middle of the night. Many parents have found themselves in the situation when a child is asking for something, but having to say, "No, I'm busy," because of other demands. It is clearly not for a lack of desire. The fire truck had long sat on a shelf in my Dad's office. As we were working through the story, that fire truck came to mind. Had I always wanted to play with it? After we made the short film I hung on to the fire truck and for a time, it sat on a shelf in the room my daughters shared. And then came the day when they asked to play with it. And what do you think I did? The ease with which you intuitively know the answer to that question ought to serve as a reminder for how your Father in heaven deeply, passionately, and unquestionably adores you, his precious child!

CLOSING THOUGHTS

Prayer is as much about listening as it is about talking. I found advice on the subject of prayer in an unlikely place. Hidden in the very practical approach to recording good audio found on the DVD resource *Sound for Film and Television* by Barry Green and David Jimmerson with Matt Gettemeier, I unearthed four ways we can improve the signal-to-noise ratio between ourselves and the Lord.

#1: Find distracting noises and silence them. If it has an on/off switch, turn it off. Find a place you can be alone with the Lord, pray, and read the Bible. Since he is omnipresent, all you have to do is find a place you won't be distracted by anything or anyone.

#2: Silence echo. Maybe hurtful or negative statements are bouncing around inside your head. Things like, "I'm no good; I'm ugly; I'm a hack." If an echo exists in a location, a good sound person will tell you to change locations. Thanks to the Lord Jesus, you are allowed to do just that by the "renewing of your mind" (Romans

12:2). If the room of your mind is filled with echo, spend time in the Word and prayer and you will change locations without moving an inch.

#3: Proximity raises the signal while lowering the noise: By deliberately making a time and place for the Lord, you will be closer to him and hear him better. James 4:8 says, "Come near to God and he will come near to you."

#4: Rejection and sensitivity combine for reach. How good is your mic? You have to be sensitive to the Lord's voice and reject all other noises in order to hear him. The more time you spend reading the Bible and in prayer, the better you'll be able to reject the voices of others and be sensitive to the Lord's. Isaiah 55:6 says, "Seek the LORD while he may be found; call on him while he is near."

Though *Sound for Film and Television* wasn't intended as a work of spiritual formation, it helped me tremendously when I discovered the spiritual lessons contained in its practical advice. The authors also say that getting good audio is 70 percent of what you see. Spiritual application: The better you hear the Lord's voice, the better your perception of everyone and everything else. And remember, even the Lord Jesus took deliberate steps to improve the signal-to-noise ratio between himself and God the Father: "Very early in the morning, while it was still dark, Jesus got up, left the house and went off to a solitary place, where he prayed" (Mark 1:35).

> I have been driven many times upon my knees
>   by the overwhelming conviction
>   that I had nowhere else to go.
>
>   Abraham Lincoln (1809 – 1865)

IN BETWEEN SESSIONS

• This week set aside a certain amount of time you will spend in prayer each day. It could be as little as five minutes. At least five days this week, spend that allocated time in prayer, and then journal about your experience.

• Say "yes." This week look for an opportunity to tell someone yes when you would normally be inclined to say no. Maybe it's someone who needs a ride, a child who wants to play, or a friend or neighbor who could use a friendly ear over a cup of coffee.

⌨ REPEAT WITH A NEW FILM OR THE SAME FILM NEXT TIME YOU MEET

THE **PARABLE** OF THE **SHREWD MANAGER**

SCRIPTURE: **LUKE 16:1–13**
FILM: *THE CAR LOT*

♡ PRAY TOGETHER

INTRODUCTION

The Parable of the Shrewd Manager examines some potentially shady business dealings. Since *Parables Remix* adapts the original parables to the modern day, what better place to explore stereotypical shady business deals than at a used car lot? The short film *The Car Lot* examines to what lengths people will go to get ahead … especially when their backs are against the wall.

In William Shakespeare's *Romeo and Juliet*, the leading man warns, "Tempt not a desperate man." It is incredible to see the ingenuity and initiative even the most irresponsible can summon when they finally recognize that something undesirable will most definitely happen unless they take action. In *The Car Lot*, after the less-than-responsible used car salesman, Trenton, is fired, he has to think fast to secure future employment. Adapting this parable to a modern context was a difficult task. Even expert theologians are divided over who the "good guys" and the "bad guys" are in the Parable of the Shrewd Manager.

👁 WATCH THE FILM *THE CAR LOT*

📖 READ THE PARABLE OF THE SHREWD MANAGER

[1] Jesus told his disciples: "There was a rich man whose manager was accused of wasting his possessions. [2] So he called him in and asked him, 'What is this I hear about you? Give an account of your management, because you cannot be manager any longer.'

[3] "The manager said to himself, 'What shall I do now? My master is taking away my job. I'm not strong enough to dig, and I'm ashamed to beg— [4] I know what I'll do so that, when I lose my job here, people will welcome me into their houses.'

[5] "So he called in each one of his master's debtors. He asked the first, 'How much do you owe my master?'

[6] "'Nine hundred gallons of olive oil,' he replied.

"The manager told him, 'Take your bill, sit down quickly, and make it four hundred and fifty.'

[7] "Then he asked the second, 'And how much do you owe?'

"'A thousand bushels of wheat,' he replied.

"He told him, 'Take your bill and make it eight hundred.'

[8] "The master commended the dishonest manager because he had acted shrewdly. For the people of this world are more shrewd in dealing with their own kind than are the people of the light. [9] I tell you, use worldly wealth to gain friends for yourselves, so that when it is gone, you will be welcomed into eternal dwellings.

[10] "Whoever can be trusted with very little can also be trusted with much, and whoever is dishonest with very little will also be dishonest with much. [11] So if you have not been trustworthy in handling worldly wealth, who will trust you with true riches? [12] And if you have not been trustworthy with someone else's property, who will give you property of your own?

[13] "No one can serve two masters. Either you will hate the one and love the other, or you will be devoted to the one and despise the other. You cannot serve both God and money."

Luke 16:1 – 13

CULTURAL BACKGROUND

This parable, on face value, is well ... confusing. In one sense, it's almost as if Jesus is condoning underhandedness. The shrewd manager, in fact, has been a problem for interpreters ever since Jesus first told this parable. The primary debate seems to center on the character of the employer. One school of thought sees him as a noble and generous man, only concerned with what's merciful. In other words, the boss has just cause to fire his dishonest employee. He even allows him to turn over his responsibilities without losing face. The dishonest employee then rewards his boss's mercy by using the extra time to endear himself to clients, all the while shamelessly counting on the master's mercy.

Once discovered, the employer has two options:

1. Refuse the sweet deals his steward offered to debtors, and look really bad in the community.

2. Write off the losses as acts of goodwill and let the scoundrel experience mercy once again.

The employer chooses the latter and, in fact, commends the shrewd employee for coming up with such a creative solution.

However, a second school of thought sees the employer and employee as equally crooked. This view takes into account the Old Testament prohibition of usury (i.e., charging interest on loans to the needy). The idea here is that the steward can discount the debts down to the original principal by removing the usurious interest charges. In this interpretation, the master cannot say anything about his steward's discount deals without exposing his own usurious schemes, so he keeps quiet and commends the scoundrel for his creativity ("shrewdness").

○ DISCUSS THE FILM AND THE ORIGINAL PARABLE

1. Of the two schools of thought—merciful manager or crooked manager—which do you think Jesus intended?

2. Based on your opinion of the manager, what would you have done if you found yourself in a similar situation?

3. Are we supposed to look at this story as an example of what to do ... or what not to do?

4. How are "shrewdness" and "creativity" similar? How are they different?

5. How could the church as a whole be more shrewd and/or creative in helping advance God's kingdom?

BEHIND THE SCENES

If you watch *The Car Lot* closely, you may notice a particular character's wardrobe mysteriously change color from one scene to the next. Any guesses? Someone in your group with a keen eye for continuity—a filmmaking term for the visual consistency of characters, their props, and surroundings from shot to shot—may have noticed. If no one noticed, that's good! It means you were paying attention to the story! (I don't think I noticed until the film was nearly completed.) The owner of the car lot, Mike, is wearing a black blazer when he is inside the building. When you see him again outside, his blazer appears to be dark brown, almost maroon.

Even though it looks like two separate sport coats, it *is* the same jacket. The day we were filming, it was so bright outside that we used multiple neutral density (ND) filters in front of the camera. ND filters are like sunglasses for a camera, reducing the light hitting the lens. Unfortunately, if you use too much ND, without an additional infrared (IR) filter, the disproportionate amount of IR getting through pollutes the image and causes color shifts.

I suppose it goes without saying that the more our vision is darkened, the less clearly we see. How fitting for a story about unclear motives and ethical dilemmas. Often, the issues we have in life and that we find in Jesus' parables do not come neatly tied with bows and ribbons.

CLOSING THOUGHTS

However you interpret the motives and actions of the characters in the Parable of the Shrewd Manager, one point you can take away is that God delights in human creativity. Creativity for kingdom purposes, not dishonest ones, is an expression of God's personality. Jesus calls for "people of the light" (his followers) to apply themselves in shrewd and creative ways, using their resources — money, possessions, and influence — to solve the problems facing this broken world. I believe the inherent value in the creativity of Christians and churches is twofold: a job well done and the edification of the local community. Take a look at one of the few accounts of an artist in the Bible and you will find these two values at work:

> "See, I have chosen Bezalel son of Uri, the son of Hur, of the tribe of Judah, and I have filled him with the Spirit of God, with wisdom, with understanding, with knowledge and with all kinds of skills — to make artistic designs for work in gold, silver and bronze, to cut and set stones, to work in wood, and to engage in all kinds of crafts." (Exodus 31:2–5)

The one word in this passage that summarizes these two values — a job well done and the edification of the local community — is *crafts*, which could also be translated *craftsmanship*. As Christians and the church continue to discuss and discover how to embrace godly creativity, we all need to remember the lessons learned from Bezalel's example: Get very good at what you do and create work that edifies your local community. Though the actual artwork Bezalel created has been lost for all time, thousands of years later he is still known for his craftsmanship. In the same way, may God fill you with skill, ability, and knowledge in your chosen creative endeavor!

> Even in literature and art, no man who bothers about originality will ever be original: whereas if you simply try to tell the truth (without caring two pence how often it has been told before) you will, nine times out of ten, become original without ever having noticed it.
>
> *Mere Christianity,*
> C. S. Lewis (1898–1963)

IN BETWEEN SESSIONS

• This week, be creative. Journal ideas you have for how your group or the church at large could do something "outside the box" with their current resources. Come prepared to share your ideas next week.

• Rewrite the Parable of the Shrewd Manager in your own context. Is there a situation at work, in your home life, or your social circle similar to this parable?

⌖ REPEAT WITH A NEW FILM OR THE SAME FILM NEXT TIME YOU MEET

THE **PARABLE** OF THE **BARREN FIG TREE**

SCRIPTURE: **LUKE 13:6–9**
FILM: *SEAN*

♡ PRAY TOGETHER

INTRODUCTION

The Parable of the Barren Fig Tree explores the intertwined themes of grace, mercy, and judgment. In the original parable it is quite likely that the vinedresser represents Jesus—the one fighting for delayed judgment on the barren fig tree. Jesus was then as he is now—perfect. So why does the teacher in the video (who likely represents Jesus) assume some of the guilt? Because "God made him who had no sin to be sin for us, so that in him we might become the righteousness of God" (2 Corinthians 5:21). When Jesus willingly gave up his life on the cross, he carried our sins and assumed our guilt. Even for those who literally had his blood on their hands Jesus pleaded, "Father, forgive them, for they do not know what they are doing" (Luke 23:34).

Like many of Jesus' parables, we don't know how this one ends. The fig tree gets one more year, but we don't know what happened to the tree once the year was up—just as we don't know what the character Sean is going to decide.

👁 WATCH THE FILM *SEAN*

📖 READ THE PARABLE OF THE BARREN FIG TREE

⁶ Then he told this parable: "A man had a fig tree growing in his vineyard, and he went to look for fruit on it but did not find any. ⁷ So he said to the man who took care of the vineyard, 'For three years now I've been coming to look for fruit on this fig tree and haven't found any. Cut it down! Why should it use up the soil?'

⁸ "'Sir,' the man replied, 'leave it alone for one more year, and I'll dig around it and fertilize it. ⁹ If it bears fruit next year, fine! If not, then cut it down.'"

Luke 13:6–9

CULTURAL BACKGROUND

The purpose of a fig tree is to bear fruit. But what do you do with something that refuses to fulfill its purpose? That's the question Jesus poses in the Parable of the Barren Fig Tree. Israel had been given a task. Sealed with God's covenant, it was called to be a "light for the Gentiles" (see Isaiah 49). The problem was that they placed their light "under a bowl" (Matthew 5:15–16), and it obscured God rather than enlightening people concerning God. Instead of spending time and energy reaching outsiders, the religious crowd was more concerned with clearly defining the beliefs and actions of an "insider."

So what's to be done? The owner of the vineyard says the barren fig tree is a waste of space, but the vinedresser intercedes for it nonetheless. Jesus is the vinedresser who's been pruning for three years ... and often to no avail. So he asks for another year to dig around and fertilize. This is the work of Jesus—offering us a second chance, one more opportunity to become fruitful under his tender care. But we must produce a response to God among the nations. This is exactly what happened in the early church era. The followers of Jesus went from a tiny minority of scared disciples to an empire-wide majority in a few hundred years. That's some fruitful growth!

Q DISCUSS THE FILM AND THE ORIGINAL PARABLE

1. It's likely that Jesus alludes to Israel as the barren fig tree in this parable. In what ways is the church not producing fruit today? In what areas is the church barren?

2. Is Jesus instructing us on being patient with others? Is there something to be learned about how we should deal with other barren fig trees?

3. In what ways have you been like the landowner (i.e., the principal in the video), ready to cut down the tree?

4. In what ways have you been like the vinedresser (i.e., the teacher in the video), pleading for mercy for another?

5. In what ways have you been like the fig tree (i.e., Sean in the video), deserving judgment, but spared?

BEHIND THE SCENES

We aren't always comfortable with nor do we fully understand the events described in the parables. Just as with life, with many of Jesus' parables, we don't know the ultimate outcome. As I shared in the introduction, I once showed *Sean*, along with a couple other *Parables Remix* short films, to a teenage couple that was blasé about God. Afterward, the boy turned to me and said, "I don't get it; what are you trying to say?" I could tell he was frustrated that the stories seemed open-ended. When I read Jesus' original stories to him from the Bible, he complained, "Well, Jesus didn't explain it either." At that moment of illumination, the boy understood. Parables make us think and ask questions. They aren't necessarily a prescription of how to live life but a description of how life in God's universe unfolds. If we really want to know what to "do," we must go to the storyteller and abide with him.

CLOSING THOUGHTS

The questions of fruitfulness remain for us today: Are we fruitful? Are we extending God's kingdom? Or are we just wasting space on the ground? Ron Sider's book *The Scandal of the Evangelical Conscience* (Baker, 2005) poses the question of the American church's fruitfulness and cannot find a single area of distinction between Christians and non-Christians in our culture.

Will the vinedresser bypass us? Or even worse ... cut us down? And just how long does his patience extend? Jesus isn't talking here about forgiveness (that was answered on the cross); he's talking about usefulness. It's entirely possible to be forgiven and remain fruitless.

And what about me? Do I serve any good purpose, or am I just taking up space?

> The trees that are slow to grow produce the best fruit.
>
> Molière (1622–1673)

IN BETWEEN SESSIONS

• This week, read John 15:1–8 at least three times and write down your thoughts and feelings about abiding in Christ and bearing fruit.

• Identify a person whom you could "dig around and fertilize." Maybe it is someone at work or school, a friend, a family member, or an acquaintance at church. Spend this week praying and journaling about a simple way you could help that person abide.

⊘ REPEAT WITH A NEW FILM OR THE SAME FILM NEXT TIME YOU MEET

THE **PARABLE** OF THE **MUSTARD SEED**

SCRIPTURE: **MARK 4:30–32**
FILM: ***CHARLIE***

♡ PRAY TOGETHER

INTRODUCTION

"Big things have small beginnings."

So says David the Android, played by Michael Fassbender, in the sci-fi film *Prometheus*, directed by Ridley Scott. In the film, David unleashes a chain of events, resulting in some very serious consequences for himself and other characters, with but one tiny drop of alien goo. Meanwhile, back in the real world, we're all aware of how the simplest ideas can go "viral" and spread across the globe in a matter of hours. Or how one small decision, to turn left instead of right, can alter the course of a person's life. Even the massive redwood tree begins as a small seed. In the Old Testament, the prophet Zechariah puts it this way: "Who dares despise the day of small things ..." (Zechariah 4:10).

In the short film *Charlie*, the father sees enormous potential in his son. However, he knows that without time and commitment, Charlie's potential will go unfulfilled. When Charlie faces adversity, he has to draw from his father's encouragement to propel him to persevere as a musician.

👁 WATCH THE FILM *CHARLIE*

📖 READ THE PARABLE OF THE MUSTARD SEED

³⁰ Again he said, "What shall we say the kingdom of God is like, or what parable shall we use to describe it? ³¹ It is like a mustard seed, which is the smallest of all seeds on earth. ³² Yet when planted, it grows and becomes the largest of all garden plants, with such big branches that the birds can perch in its shade."

Mark 4:30–32

CULTURAL BACKGROUND

Jesus wasn't the package that the teachers of the law were expecting for their Messiah. He was conceived before his mother and father were married, born in a stable, and hailed from a backwater village — a poor laborer with no academic credentials or political influence. And he was hardly the sparkling warrior who would vanquish the Romans.

So when Jesus announced the inauguration of "the kingdom of God" in his ministry as the promised Messiah, the teachers of the law were understandably underwhelmed. Jesus told the Parable of the Mustard Seed to illustrate how God's kingdom works. It begins small and unimpressively, but with time, nurture, and commitment, the diminutive seed can turn into an impressive, mature plant. So, too, with the kingdom. Immediately following this parable, Mark's gospel goes on to say, "With many similar parables Jesus spoke the word to them, as much as they could understand. He did not say anything to them without using a parable. But when he was alone with his own disciples, he explained everything" (vv. 33–34). Here is the same principle at work. Anyone within earshot could hear a parable. It was later, in a personal relationship with Jesus that his disciples had the opportunity for lasting growth.

⊂⟩ DISCUSS THE FILM AND THE ORIGINAL PARABLE

1. In what ways did Jesus fail to meet the expectations of the religious leaders of his day?

2. Where does the church today fail to meet the expectations of your friends, family, and neighbors?

3. Where have you seen great things that came in small or unimpressive packages?

4. What endeavors have you given up on because your early results were unimpressive?

5. If you could see your gifts from God's perspective, what pursuit(s) would you persevere in?

BEHIND THE SCENES

In making *Parables Remix*, it often felt as though the eighteen parables chose us instead of the other way around. Such was the case with *Charlie*, when it seemed that the Mark 4 parable called to us in the sounds of a saxophone. The name of the film is a tribute to the famed saxophonist Charlie Parker. We even filmed at the Phoenix Jazz Club in Kansas City, near where the jazz legend was born and raised, and shot the opening scene in front of the Charlie Parker Memorial close to downtown. We shot an additional scene at the memorial that did not make it into the final film. It is a simple wedding scene, in which all you can see is Charlie, May, and a minister standing in front of the statue. It makes you wonder if Jesus had certain "scenes" he had to cut from his parables. These are the sort of personal details we can only learn by growing in a more intimate relationship with the storyteller.

CLOSING THOUGHTS

The Bible tells us that God has created each human being with gifts of enormous potential (Romans 12; 1 Corinthians 12). Unfortunately, our potential often goes unrealized due to impatience and inconsistency, the exact opposites of time and commitment. In Mark 4:26–29, Jesus tells another parable about a seed:

> He also said, "This is what the kingdom of God is like. A man scatters seed on the ground. Night and day, whether he sleeps or gets up, the seed sprouts and grows, though he does not know how. All by itself the soil produces grain—first the stalk, then the head, then the full kernel in the head. As soon as the grain is ripe, he puts the sickle to it, because the harvest has come."

The seed in both of these parables is *committed* to growth over *time*. The kingdom functions in the very same way God intends us to function: commitment over time.

God wants us to remember the mustard seed when our spirits are lagging, or when we lose confidence in our potential. God also wants us to remember this principle when God's kingdom seems small or unimpressive in our culture or in our lives. If we remain committed over time, abiding in him through thick and thin, we will grow and bear fruit. Jesus' kingdom is growing and will one day completely mature into an impressive plant — but you and I must not be discouraged by its seemingly insignificant start.

> So be it, Lord; Thy throne shall never,
> Like earth's proud empires, pass away:
> Thy kingdom stands, and grows forever,
> Till all Thy creatures own Thy sway.
>
> *The Day Thou Gavest, Lord, Is Ended,*
> John Ellerton (1826 – 1893)

IN BETWEEN SESSIONS

- This week, write down two or three other big things that have small beginnings. When they come to mind, write down your thoughts and feelings about the areas in your life that the Lord is currently growing.

- Who in your life needs to be encouraged by this mustard seed principle? Commit to contact the person this week, share the Mark 4 parable, and, most importantly, listen to what he or she has to say in response.

REPEAT WITH A NEW FILM OR THE SAME FILM NEXT TIME YOU MEET

THE **PARABLE** OF THE **WHEAT** AND THE **WEEDS**

SCRIPTURE: **MATTHEW 13:24–30**
FILM: *TOGETHER*

♡ PRAY TOGETHER

INTRODUCTION

Don't you wish the world came with labels — GOOD SEED … BAD SEED? It'd be so much easier if we could get the wheat far from the weeds right at the start. But Jesus says that if we attempt to remove the weeds now, we endanger the wheat. For the time being, we are to "let both grow together."

The short film *Together* is a picture of that painful reality. Gary is a dad whose alcoholism has had a devastating influence on his family. We catch up with him as he is trying to change things by keeping a promise and throwing a birthday party for his daughter. At the same time Gary is putting up with his brother's "weedlike" influence — he wants Gary to continue a tradition of giving alcohol for birthdays … this time for Gary's daughter. Gary endures temptation, but his daughter and brother let alcohol get the best of them, with unfortunate results. Being "together" means having to tolerate the bad influences of the here and now alongside the good, and trusting that God will sort it all out at a later time.

👁 WATCH THE FILM *TOGETHER*

📖 READ THE PARABLE OF THE WHEAT AND THE WEEDS

[24] Jesus told them another parable: "The kingdom of heaven is like a man who sowed good seed in his field. [25] But while everyone was sleeping, his enemy came and sowed weeds among the wheat, and went away. [26] When the wheat sprouted and formed heads, then the weeds also appeared.

[27] "The owner's servants came to him and said, 'Sir, didn't you sow good seed in your field? Where then did the weeds come from?'

[28] "'An enemy did this,' he replied.

"The servants asked him, 'Do you want us to go and pull them up?'

[29] "'No,' he answered, 'because while you are pulling the weeds, you may uproot the wheat with them. [30] Let both grow together until the harvest. At that time I will tell the harvesters: First collect the weeds and tie them in bundles to be burned; then gather the wheat and bring it into my barn.'"

Matthew 13:24–30

CULTURAL BACKGROUND

In Jesus' day, "tares" (rendered "weeds" in the NIV) were noxious little weeds also known as "darnel." The seed looked similar to the wheat seed, so it often got mixed with the wheat accidentally. It also appears that immature darnel sprouts looked a lot like wheat as well, making it hard to weed the crop in the early stages. This meant waiting until the crop matured to do the weeding.

This parable gives us a glimpse of how evil works. When confronted with the weeds that have been sown among the wheat, the master in the story simply states, "An enemy did this." No great discussion over why or how. The explanation of evil in the parable is only a simple admission that the master has an enemy, and an acknowledgment that his enemy was proactive enough to sow destruction. The desire of the zealous workers to pull out the weeds, thereby destroying the crop, may have been part of the enemy's plan all along. This idea of well-meaning do-gooders wreaking havoc by their efforts to remove the effects of evil in the world is developed in Robert Farrar Capon's discussion of the parable in his book *Parables of the Kingdom*. Simply put, "The road to hell is paved with good intentions."

DISCUSS THE FILM AND THE ORIGINAL PARABLE

1. How has the church throughout history failed to heed Jesus' teaching with respect to the wheat and the weeds?

2. How do we tell the wheat from the weeds today? Are they easy to distinguish?

3. Why does God allow this world to be filled with such a mixed bag of wheat and weeds?

4. Why is it so hard for us to wait for the "harvest"?

5. How, according to Jesus, are we to act toward those whom we perceive as weeds in our lives?

BEHIND THE SCENES

One of the most common questions we get about the *Parables Remix* short films is, "Are those real actors?" It's hard not to respond in jest: "No, they're actually animated." But if we understand the question correctly, the answer is, more often than not, "No, they are not *professional* actors." Many amateur or first-time actors have given performances in the *Parables Remix* films. Some of the actors came from work in the theater. Some of them are merely portraying on screen their real-life vocation—as in the case of *Together* when the policeman in the final scene was played by an off-duty officer with a bona fide police cruiser. And some of the actors are closely related to co-creators of the series! Both of our parents have made cameo appearances in at least one of the short films. As a matter of fact, there are a handful of professional actors in the films as well. Most likely, you won't recognize any of them.

Similar to Jesus' original parables, the stories we strive to tell are about everyday people and events. John Schimke, the co-creator of *Parables Remix* and director of all eighteen short films, has done a superb job of drawing out natural, authentic, and high-quality performances from a wide range of talent.

CLOSING THOUGHTS

Why is evil often the most intriguing element in stories? Some say it is because our sinful nature gets so tantalized by the deeds of darkness that we can't get enough. Others say it is a sign that things are getting worse. I believe it's a combination of both, multiplied by a misunderstanding of the advancement of God's kingdom as taught in Jesus' parables.

In the West, many believe that the cosmic struggle between good and evil is an extrapolation of the law of entropy. If good doesn't respond to evil, things will continue to get worse. But entropy-focused morality lowers the bar, makes us throw in the towel and think, "Someone is bound to steal it sooner or later anyway." Jesus, on the other hand, teaches us that the kingdom of heaven has already arrived. His resurrection is the firstfruits and things will get better and better even as they get worse and worse.

In the Parable of the Wheat and the Weeds, the farmer whose field has been sown with weeds by "an enemy" says, "Let both grow together ..." It's tempting to want to weed the world of "tares." The problem is that it's hard to distinguish between them and the good stuff. This means we must leave justice (weeding) to God. We must trust that he'll take the evil ones away one future day, which allows us to drop the sickle today. Our job is to try to be good soil for the seed right now (as Jesus illustrated in the Parable of the Sower). Therefore we shouldn't be surprised by the presence of "hypocrites" in the church; there is a real enemy who comes in the middle of the night and sows bad seed.

We seem alike when thus we meet,
Strangers might think we all are wheat;
But to the Lord's all-searching eyes,
Each heart appears without disguise.

Carol of the Wheat and Tares, verse 4,
John Newton (1705–1807)

IN BETWEEN SESSIONS

• This week, journal a brief history of your life in chapters covering five to ten years each. Write one to three ways you were wheat in each chapter and one to three ways you were a weed. Identify one or two influential people in each chapter who were either wheat or weeds.

- How can you be wheat this week? Wheat is intended to be fruitful. And we know we can only bear fruit by remaining in an abiding relationship with Jesus (John 15). Commit to spend at least one hour this week "abiding" with Jesus. This may look different for everyone, but the result is the same: "By their fruit you will recognize them" (Matthew 7:20).

⌖ REPEAT WITH A NEW FILM OR THE SAME FILM NEXT TIME YOU MEET

THE **PARABLE** OF THE **WISE** AND **FOOLISH BUILDERS**

SCRIPTURE: **LUKE 6:46–49**
FILM: ***WISE/FOOLISH***

♡ PRAY TOGETHER

INTRODUCTION

Like water, it's normal for humans to look for the path of least resistance. We call this procrastination. Psychologist M. Scott Peck says that laziness was part of our original sin. We could've eaten "any fruit in the garden," but instead we chose to eat from the one tree from which God forbade us to eat.

In the film *Wise/Foolish*, a college student procrastinates on a crucial term paper because of the distraction of a new boyfriend. She is like the fool in Jesus' parable who chose the path of least resistance by building a beach house (clearly the superior hangout pad) instead of putting in the hard work upfront by building on a rock foundation. More time … more labor … more cost! Jesus points out that the wisdom of a rock-solid foundation only becomes apparent in a storm. All of a sudden, wisdom is vindicated. The foolish student in the film learns this painful lesson when she gets expelled from school after taking an ill-advised shortcut. Because she didn't invest the time and energy earlier, her foundation didn't hold in a moment of crisis.

👁 WATCH THE FILM *WISE/FOOLISH*

📖 READ THE PARABLE OF THE WISE AND FOOLISH BUILDERS

⁴⁶ "Why do you call me, 'Lord, Lord,' and do not do what I say? ⁴⁷ As for everyone who comes to me and hears my words and puts them into practice, I will show you what they are like. ⁴⁸ They are like a man building a house, who dug down deep and laid the foundation on rock. When a flood came, the torrent struck that house but could not shake it, because it was well built. ⁴⁹ But the one who hears my words and does not put them into practice is like a man who built a house on the ground without a foundation. The moment the torrent struck that house, it collapsed and its destruction was complete."

Luke 6:46–49

CULTURAL BACKGROUND

The basics of building have changed very little since the days of Jesus. Wise construction always has been about building on a solid foundation. In Jesus' time, this would have meant digging deep enough to find rock. The context of this parable seems to be the Palestinian wadi—a ravine with steep sides that drains away the water during downpours. In Jesus' parable, all is well with both houses until the storms come. Winter storms in Israel could produce significant flooding, as the wadi banks channeled fierce floodwaters away from the villages. It's at this point that the two buildings distinguish themselves: The homes of the wise could hold fast in these crisis moments, but no such luck was found for the path-of-least-resistance builders. The homes built on sandy earth would quickly give way to the power of the floodwaters.

Jesus guarantees that the storms will come. He says, "When a flood came," not "if." Life on this planet is inherently risky and full of challenge. Nonetheless, Jesus offers us a way to weather any storm: "I have told you these things, so that in me you may have peace. In this world you will have trouble. But take heart! I have overcome the world" (John 16:33).

Q DISCUSS THE FILM AND THE ORIGINAL PARABLE

1. What do you suppose is our motivation for procrastination and/or taking the path of least resistance?

2. What one "wise" thing should you include in your life foundation today?

3. What percentage of people in America who call themselves "Christians" do you think are like the wise builder? Like the foolish builder?

4. What are the things that distract us from digging deeper and founding our lives upon bedrock?

5. If you could identify one area of "shifting sand" in your life, what would it be?

BEHIND THE SCENES

The best part of filming *Wise/Foolish* was bringing an outrageous story to life. Some people may find it hard to believe that Stephanie would actually give her friend, Eve, a paper and say, "Just use it as a guide." But it happens to be a true story and I happen to be one of the two characters. It was the very end of the second semester of my freshman year and a big paper was due. There was a concert I really wanted to go to, but I needed to get the paper completed. My best friend let me look at his paper to see how he tackled the project. Pretty soon, I was retyping each sentence in my own words. However, in the true story, I never did get caught. Maybe that is what compelled me to write the script: a little delayed justice. The way that I approach screenwriting most often is I get an idea for a story, like this one that happened to be true. Then I'll put a song on repeat, sometimes the same one for hours and hours, and just write. I can even remember listening to a song on repeat when I was retyping that paper in college!

CLOSING THOUGHTS

Close to 80 percent of Americans call themselves "Christian" and yet recent studies show no areas of distinction between "Christians" and "non-Christians." Not in personal morality, not in social ethics, not in family life, not even in giving. Could it be that we have a form of Christianity that's been built on shifting sand instead of a firm foundation? Jesus told his followers that they had a choice of two paths: the path of discipline, which often schedules the tough stuff upfront … or the path of procrastination and least resistance, which schedules the fun stuff upfront and remains oblivious to the coming weather.

There's an often quoted proverb about the foolish that says, "As a dog returns to its vomit, so fools repeat their folly" (Proverbs 26:11). For some people, it is relatively easy to see how making good decisions benefits us and bad decisions harm others and ourselves. Avoiding foolishness is rarely the problem. However, the very next verse in Proverbs states, "Do you see a person wise in their own eyes? There is more hope for a fool than for them" (Proverbs 26:12). We also must not be too quick to become "wise in our own eyes." Measuring ourselves against others or even focusing solely on our behavior will not get us through the torrents in life. The only sure foundation is abiding in Jesus.

> His oath, His covenant, His blood,
> Support me in the whelming flood.
> When all around my soul gives way,
> He then is all my Hope and Stay.

> On Christ the solid Rock I stand,
> All other ground is sinking sand;
> All other ground is sinking sand.

> *My Hope Is Built* on *Nothing Less*, verse 3
> and refrain, Edward Mote (1797–1874)

IN THE COMING DAYS

- This week, take time to identify any areas in your life where you have been building foolishly. Also, identify any areas where you have been "wise in your own eyes." Then make a third list that identifies areas where you are building on the firm foundation of abiding in Jesus. Compare and contrast the three lists.

- Use your third list as a starting point for a "blueprint" of your house. Draw a large rock—this is Jesus—and then draw your house on top of the rock. Use your list to inspire the foundation, the four walls, and roof. Do you have enough for an entire house or are there areas in need of repair?

✪ REPEAT WITH A NEW FILM OR THE SAME FILM NEXT TIME YOU MEET

The Path to the Cross Discovery Guide with DVD

Five Faith Lessons

Ray Vander Laan with Stephen and Amanda Sorenson

In this five-lesson DVD with Discussion Guide, filmed in hi-definition on location throughout Israel, Vander Laan takes the story of the Bible full circle—reminding viewers of the Exodus and culminating with Jesus' death and resurrection.

God's story culminates with the intense devotion of his people in this eleventh volume of the Faith Lessons series. Discover how their passionate faith prepares the way for Jesus and his ultimate act of obedience and sacrifice at the cross. Then, be challenged in your own life to live as they did—by every word that comes from the mouth of God.

Five sessions include:

1. The Way of the Essenes
2. The Way of John the Baptist
3. Into the Desert to Be Tested
4. The Last Passover
5. The Fifth Cup: Our Way of Hope

The Prodigal God Curriculum Kit

Finding Your Place at the Table

Timothy Keller

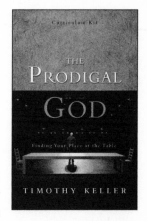

In this compelling six-session DVD study, pastor and bestselling author Tim Keller presents a new way of looking at this well-known parable.

Where most teaching focuses just on the younger "wayward" son, Dr. Keller challenges us to consider both the role of the elder brother and the father as well.

Even Jesus began his parable with "a man had two sons" so, you see, the story is not just about the younger son who leaves home and squanders his inheritance before eventually returning home.

The story is as much about the elder brother as the younger, and as much about the father as the sons. To this end, Dr. Keller contends that the story might better be called "Two Lost Sons."

In six sessions your group will explore the prodigal who spent until he had nothing left, the self-righteous and offended elder son, and the father who forgave with reckless abandon.

And in it all, your group will learn the love of the heavenly Father who lavishes his love upon his children and welcomes us back into his loving arms.

The kit contains one (1) each of the following: *The Prodigal God* DVD, *The Prodigal God Discussion Guide*, *The Prodigal God* book, and the "Getting Started Guide."

Available in stores and online!

Share Your Thoughts

With the Author: Your comments will be forwarded to the author when you send them to *zauthor@zondervan.com*.

With Zondervan: Submit your review of this book by writing to *zreview@zondervan.com*.

Free Online Resources at
www.zondervan.com

Zondervan AuthorTracker: Be notified whenever your favorite authors publish new books, go on tour, or post an update about what's happening in their lives at www.zondervan.com/authortracker.

Daily Bible Verses and Devotions: Enrich your life with daily Bible verses or devotions that help you start every morning focused on God. Visit www.zondervan.com/newsletters.

Free Email Publications: Sign up for newsletters on Christian living, academic resources, church ministry, fiction, children's resources, and more. Visit www.zondervan.com/newsletters.

Zondervan Bible Search: Find and compare Bible passages in a variety of translations at www.zondervanbiblesearch.com.

Other Benefits: Register to receive online benefits like coupons and special offers, or to participate in research.